PITMAN'S
Broadway Theatre at 100

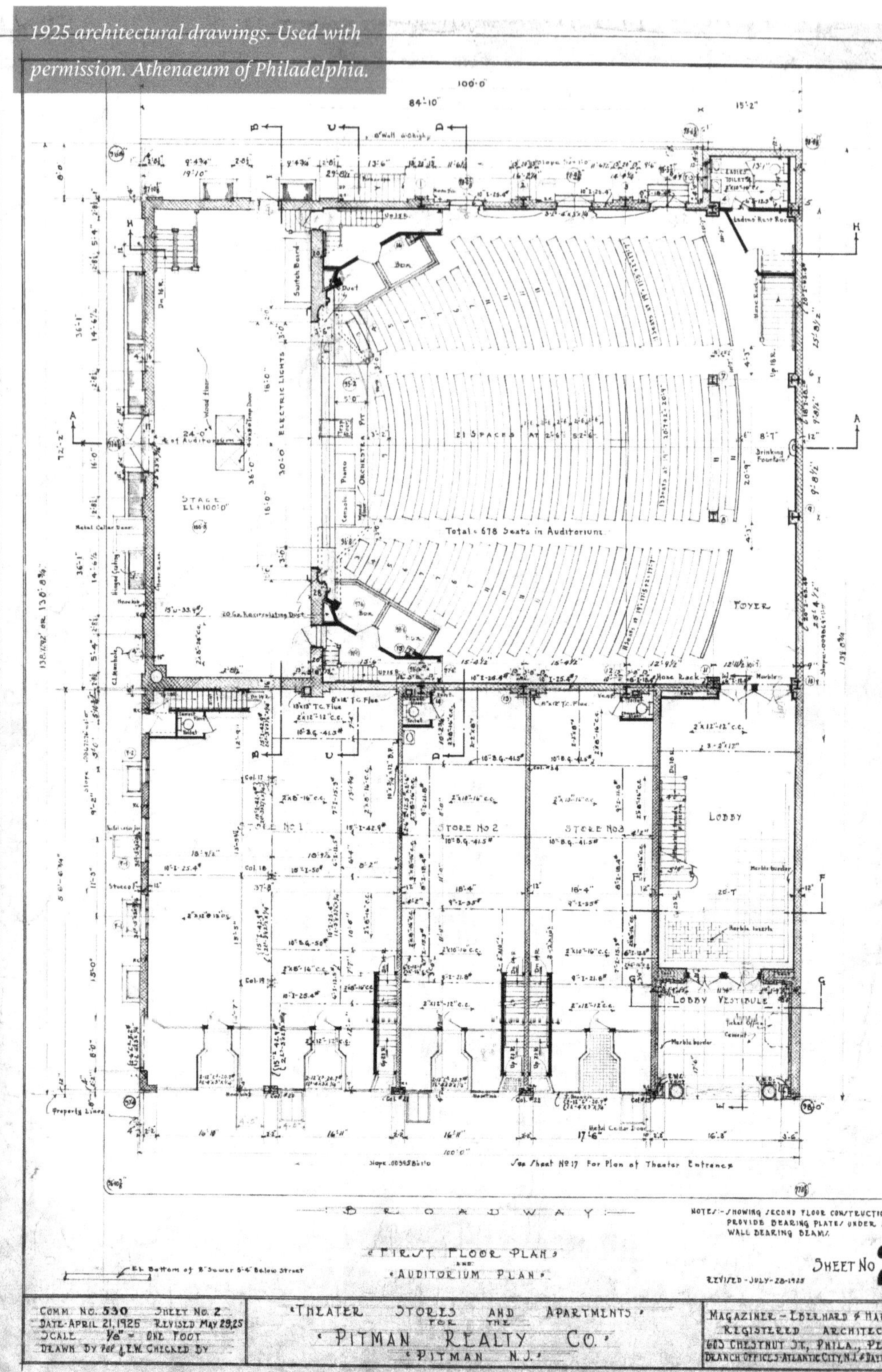
FIRST FLOOR PLAN
AND
AUDITORIUM PLAN
B R O A D W A Y
Total = 678 Seats in Auditorium
STAGE
STORE No 1
STORE No 2
STORE No 3
LOBBY
LOBBY VESTIBULE
FOYER
SHEET No 2
NOTES:- SHOWING SECOND FLOOR CONSTRUCTION
PROVIDE BEARING PLATES UNDER ALL
WALL BEARING BEAMS
REVISED - JULY-28-1925
COMM. No. 530   SHEET No. 2
DATE-APRIL 21, 1925   REVISED MAY 29, 25
SCALE 1/8" = ONE FOOT
DRAWN BY J.E.W. CHECKED BY
THEATER   STORES   AND   APARTMENTS
FOR THE
PITMAN REALTY CO.
PITMAN N.J.
MAGAZINER - EBERHARD & HARRIS
REGISTERED ARCHITECTS
603 CHESTNUT ST, PHILA, PENN
BRANCH OFFICES-ATLANTIC CITY, N.J. & DAYTONA
THEATRE = 420,000 CU. FT.
STORES & APARTMENTS

Advance Praise for 'Pitman's Broadway Theatre at 100'

"Eldredge's history uses a combination of anecdotal examples, biographical detail and broader historical context, including details of local politics, to create a sweeping narrative of the Broadway. There are many specific details that make the history feel especially vivid and the many interviews help to personalize the events of its story further. A thorough and deeply felt story of a New Jersey landmark."

— **Kirkus Reviews**

"'Time capsule' may be an overused term, but it suits this generous book. Richard Eldredge has re-created his hometown with exacting and entertaining detail so descriptive that the scenes are nearly tangible. He has reassembled the lives of townspeople through the decades who are ambitious, sometimes philanthropic, perennial dreamers. Many of us live with one foot propping open the door to easy nostalgia. But Eldredge has not written a sentimental guidebook idealizing small-town life. Readers will be rewarded with a richly nuanced experience which risks a pun: The book is cinematic.

Though it invites us specifically to Pitman, New Jersey, that town is simply a wonderful lens. The history of the Broadway Theatre opens a dialogue about the universal need for every human village to build and protect its story-telling hub. Haven't we all at one time or another lived in a small city which grappled with a way to save its old movie theatre — or in other instances its architecture, culture, arts scene? This book expresses gratitude to those magnanimous restorers of our palatial and exuberant civic past, who — as Eldredge himself has done on these pages — resurrect the very heart and soul of community."

— **Susan O'Dell Underwood**, author of "Genesis Road"

"It's hard to describe what the Broadway Theatre means to the Borough of Pitman. The theatre has always been a center of activity and has drawn people to support our up-town restaurants and shops. The theatre has evolved over the years to meet the times — from vaudeville and movies to movies and live music and now live theatre and music but has always remained an essential part of our community by hosting many first dates, movies with friends and family, pageants, after prom events, children's theatre and on and on. We are fortunate to have had the Broadway Theatre be a part of our lives through it all."

— **Debra Moore Higbee**, Pitman Historical Museum

Photo from the collection of Ralph J. Richards Jr.

PITMAN'S BROADWAY THEATRE at 100

The Story of a Beloved Landmark and the New Jersey Town That Saved It

by

Richard L. Eldredge

Ardmore Avenue
PUBLISHING

ATLANTA
2025

Paperback ISBN: 979-8-9912060-1-3
Library of Congress Control Number: 2025913308

This book is a work of nonfiction. The events are portrayed as accurately as possible. The views expressed in this book are solely those of the author and the individuals quoted.

Many of the photographs reproduced in this publication originate from archival collections and personal contributions, with several dating back to the early 1900s. Every effort has been made to trace copyright holders and secure permissions where applicable. These images are used under the protections of U.S. copyright law, including public domain and fair use provisions where relevant. All rights to reproduced images remain with their respective copyright holders unless otherwise noted.

Cover and Book Design: Paolo Aguila. Typography set in Crimson Pro by Sebastian Kosch, BioRhyme by Aoife Mooney and Broadway (digitized by Monotype). All fonts licensed via Google Fonts under open source terms.

Copyediting by E.A. Axelberg

Printed by Ardmore Avenue Publishing, in the United States of America

First printing edition 2025

Ardmore Avenue Publishing
www.ardmoreavenuepublishing.com

To my aunt, Joan Schaeffer Eldredge and the memory of my mother, Barbara Schaeffer Eldredge, sisters who grew up going to the Broadway and passed along a love of the theatre to their children.

And to the people of Pitman, past, present and future. You are the reason this book exists.

BROADWAY

Table of Contents

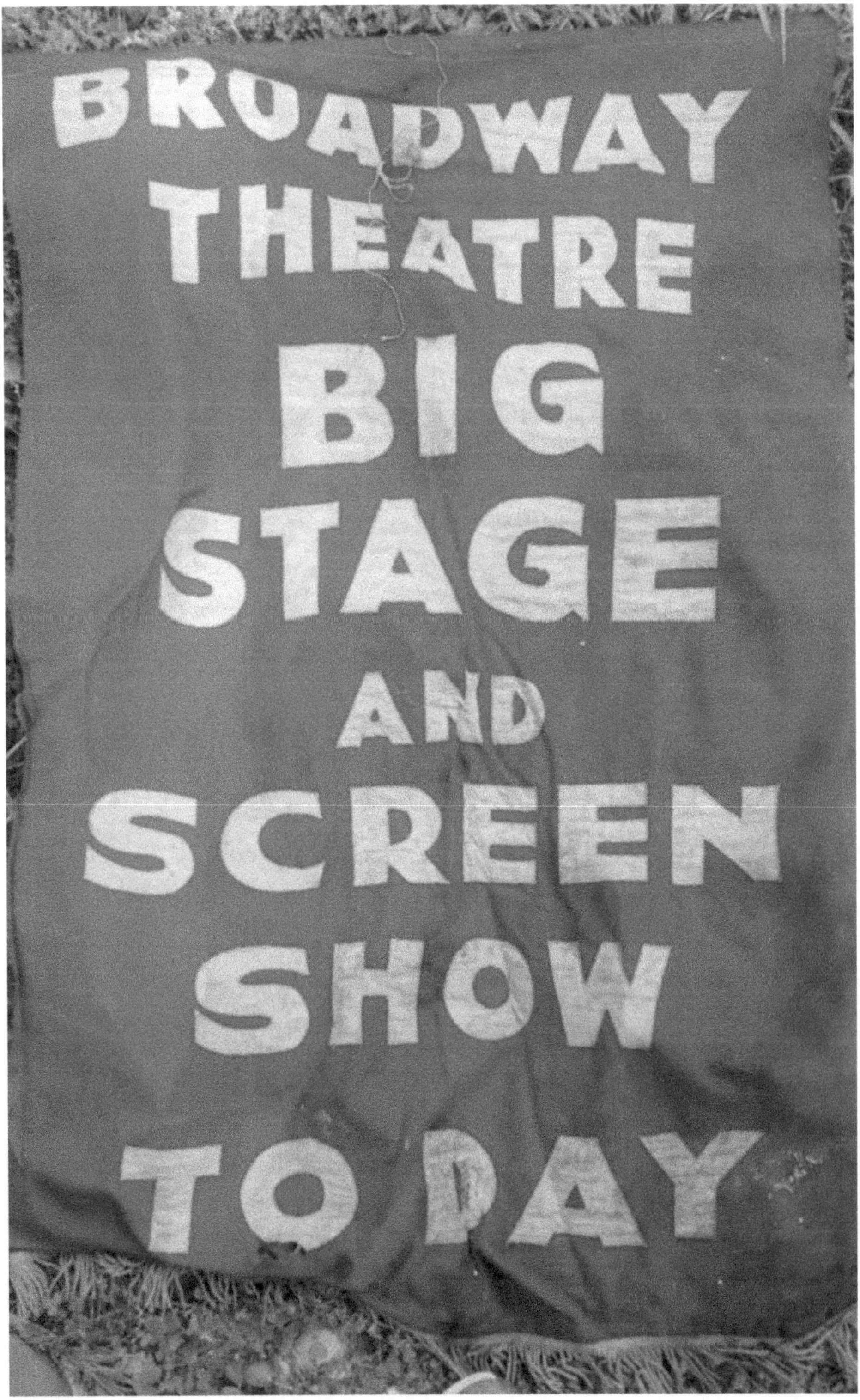

BROADWAY
THEATRE
BIG
STAGE
AND
SCREEN
SHOW
TO DAY

BROADWAY
BROADWAY

A WEEKEND FULL OF ENTERTAINMENT
BROADWAY
BROADWAY
Martini's

Author's Note

The seeds of this book may well have germinated in the spring of 1977. As a sixth grader at Pitman Middle School I knew two things — (1.) I excelled at reading and writing; (2.) My complete absence of athletic prowess often resulted in a trip to the nurse's office. Noting my aptitude for writing, Claudia Cuddy, the advisor for the Pitman Middle School Message newspaper, suggested I try my hand at reporting. Marsha Hahn, the school's media center director was equally encouraging as I devoured issues of the Gloucester County Times, Courier-Post and the Philadelphia Inquirer, along with film strips, 8mm films and almost every new book put on the shelf. Using one of Pitman Middle's new electric cassette tape recorders and a small handheld microphone, I interviewed my classmates about the school's media center. The result, "Library Likes," was written on sheets of loose leaf three-ring binder notebook paper in my upstairs bedroom on Ardmore Avenue. Published in the March 8, 1977 Pitman Middle School Message, it became my first-ever bylined newspaper story. Thanks to Mrs. Cuddy and Mrs. Hahn and their encouragement nearly 50 years ago, I've been reporting ever since.

That same year, on my way to McCowan Memorial Library after school, I crashed my bike, fracturing my arm. The resulting cast yielded two unexpected dividends. For weeks, Coach Ruf excused me from gym class, where my specialty was taking a large red rubber ball to the face during dodge ball. Coach Ruf would scribble out a hall pass and send me upstairs to the auditorium. There, one grade at a time over a period of three weeks, the sixth, seventh and eighth graders were being introduced to the 1964 Best Picture Academy Award-winning musical "My Fair Lady." It was the first time I ever got to watch a movie three times with three different audiences. Sitting in the back of the theatre, I studied the reactions, music, script, acting, costumes, set design and cinematography — tools I still use today as an arts reporter working in Atlanta.

Library   Likes

By Richard Eldredge

On a dull Friday afternoon in January, a library club member turned reporter and asked the people in the library what the library meant to them.

Andrea Rose: I think it's a useful place and I like it.
Lisa Lewis: Well I think it's nice that people can come and use the A.V. materials and read.
Mrs. Hahn: Ahhh! Are you recording???sigh! Should I cry? Sigh! Joy! pure Joy! Wonderful Joy! there's Richard crawling on the floor plugging in his tape recorder and Troy unplugging it. Isn't this joy?
Patti Nailor: Nothing much. Books and A.V. equipment.
Dawn Hasher: A place to read and study and do your homework.
Susan Cancglin: It means studying and a place where you can come and lounge. I mean, browse around.
Alan Karas: It means you can come and listen to records and listen to tapes and read books.
Lisa Shockley: It means books and magazines and it means you have time to fool around.
Clint Lovell: It's a place where you can go and study and do your work, etc.
Jill Debus: A place to work after school. Also a place to get information for history projects (Mrs. V. beware!
Kim Morton: Quiet studying and nobody bothers you.
Kim Morrison: Huh?
Bob Crothewski: "Nothing!"
Troy Lawrence: Leave me alone. I'm reading Shakespeare!!
John Newcomb: Rest and Relaxation
Jenny Rowland: Not You!!

And so concludes our so-called survey!

As a kid growing up in Pitman, if I wasn't at the library or the comic book racks at Pownall's or the J&K Market, I was at the Broadway Theatre watching every movie my weekly allowance could finance. Like many of you, the Broadway represents an irreplaceable piece of my childhood. Having the opportunity to report and write a book about its history has been one of the greatest gifts of my career. More importantly, working on this book has reconnected me with cherished classmates, neighbors and old family friends while introducing me to many new Pitmanites. For example, in my final interview with the Broadway's current owner, Peter Slack, I discovered he was one of the kids sliding into third on the Little League field visible through our kitchen window as I helped my mother dry dishes after dinner. Likewise, Peter discovered that his assistant of the last 25 years was my next-door neighbor and babysitter growing up. Small world indeed.

The overwhelming kindness, help and support I've received from the people of Pitman throughout this project have served to remind me of the values, first learned here in childhood, that I've carried with me through my life. Or as Pitman Mayor Michael Razze stated in an interview for the book, "Neighbors show up to help and support each other here. It's just what you do in Pitman."

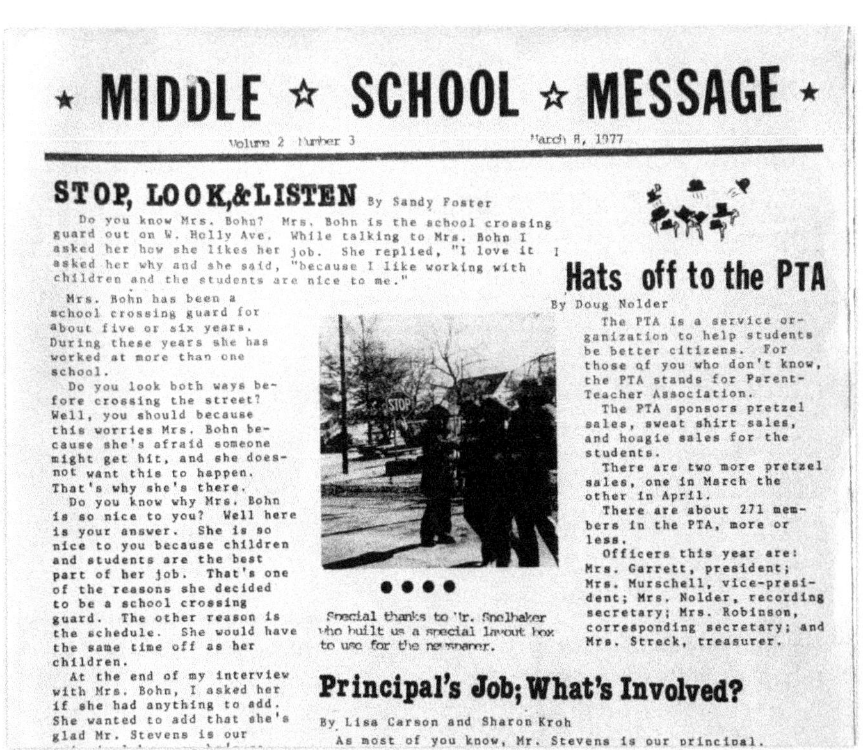

★ MIDDLE ☆ SCHOOL ☆ MESSAGE ★

Volume 2 Number 3   March 8, 1977

STOP, LOOK,&LISTEN By Sandy Foster

Do you know Mrs. Bohn? Mrs. Bohn is the school crossing guard out on W. Holly Ave. While talking to Mrs. Bohn I asked her how she likes her job. She replied, "I love it I asked her why and she said, "because I like working with children and the students are nice to me."

Mrs. Bohn has been a school crossing guard for about five or six years. During these years she has worked at more than one school.

Do you look both ways before crossing the street? Well, you should because this worries Mrs. Bohn because she's afraid someone might get hit, and she doesn't want this to happen. That's why she's there.

Do you know why Mrs. Bohn is so nice to you? Well here is your answer. She is so nice to you because children and students are the best part of her job. That's one of the reasons she decided to be a school crossing guard. The other reason is the schedule. She would have the same time off as her children.

At the end of my interview with Mrs. Bohn, I asked her if she had anything to add. She wanted to add that she's glad Mr. Stevens is our

Special thanks to Mr. Snelbaker who built us a special layout box to use for the newspaper.

Hats off to the PTA

By Doug Nolder

The PTA is a service organization to help students be better citizens. For those of you who don't know, the PTA stands for Parent-Teacher Association.

The PTA sponsors pretzel sales, sweat shirt sales, and hoagie sales for the students.

There are two more pretzel sales, one in March the other in April.

There are about 271 members in the PTA, more or less.

Officers this year are: Mrs. Garrett, president; Mrs. Murschell, vice-president; Mrs. Nolder, recording secretary; Mrs. Robinson, corresponding secretary; and Mrs. Streck, treasurer.

Principal's Job; What's Involved?

By Lisa Carson and Sharon Kroh

As most of you know, Mr. Stevens is our principal.

Attempting to tackle 100 years of history is a sizable task. Whenever possible, primary sources (e.g. first-person interviews, published newspaper accounts, historical archives, real estate records, signed contracts) have been utilized to bring you the most factual account of the Broadway's storied history. That said, as Pitman historian Harold F. Wilson noted in the preface to his 1955 "Cottagers and Commuters: A History of Pitman," "Without a doubt some errors have found their way into the book, but every effort has been made to keep it as accurate as possible."

Please accept this book as a token of my appreciation for everything this "Small Town With a Big Heart" has given me throughout my life. Thank you.

R.L.E.
May 19, 2025

BROADWAY

Dr. Henry H. Carr's residence on Broadway, the current site of the Broadway Theatre. Used with permission. Gloucester County Historical Society.

Foreword

This book is about people, places, churches and planning for the future. Pitman began, like so many other communities, with the Methodist Church and the train both coming through the area, then a part of Mantua Township, now the Borough of Pitman. It was not long after the Pitman Grove was created that it broke away from Mantua Township and formed its own small borough inside of the township.

But this book is more about the individuals who made up the community of Pitman and their farsighted thinking, which would help make Pitman what it is today. If we turn back the pages of yesteryear, we find that Pitman's business district was gradually developing along the Broadway area and its residences were outside of that area — with one exception. The very large stone residence that sat where the Broadway Theatre sits today.

That was my grandfather Dr. Henry H. Carr's residence.

Dr. Carr, a recent graduate of Hahnemann Medical College in Philadelphia, born and raised in Richwood, eventually moved his successful practice to Pitman. The home he created on Broadway accommodated not only his office but hospital-type rooms for those who needed help, as there was no hospital in the area. This beautiful home of stone was accompanied by a stable behind the house where initially he kept horses and, later on, a Hudson automobile.

Ultimately the house was torn down after Dr. Carr died and my grandmother sold the property. In its place, a theatre was built. That theatre, the Broadway, still exists today. There are key people involved in that who should be identified and praised for their efforts. Among these were Ralph Wilkins, who originally managed and owned the theatre. Under Ralph's guidance, the theatre brought to the borough a new form of entertainment that was gradually accepted and it also brought business to Broadway, the street. Pitman thereafter grew until it reached its present size.

Along the way, as in all growing communities, there were problems. But there were also many forward-thinking people, such as the Honorable Jack Robbins, mayor of Pitman, followed by Mayor Robert F. Shoemaker. It was Mayor Shoemaker who determined that the Pitman Grove should be restored, as it had fallen into severe disrepair. With that came a new form of energy for the community and its downtown.

Throughout the century, the theatre changed hands multiple times. And like the rest of Pitman's business district, the Broadway Theatre has navigated both economic downturns and the whims of a changing world. We should all thank Peter Slack, the theatre's current owner, for his forward thinking. Prosperity has returned not only to the theatre but to all of Broadway.

Thanks to this foresight, Pitman has developed into the community we know today. We should reach back and thank all the people who were involved in preparing for the future.

Being a member of the Carr family, I have been asked to say just a few words and perhaps thank those who went before us — the people who created our community which we love so well. As the Broadway celebrates its centennial, we can thank the visionary individuals who continue to look toward the promise of the future and not to the past.

Warren H. Carr,
Counselor-at-Law
Creese and Carr

Photo of the original Pitman Train Station. From the author's collection.

Introduction

For a century, the Broadway Theatre of Pitman has stood as more than just a building of brick and stone — it has been the beating heart of our community. Since its grand opening in 1926, the theatre has served as a window into the evolving spirit, culture and economy of Pitman. As we look back on 100 years of its remarkable history, we don't just celebrate the performances, the films or the stars who graced its stage — we celebrate the story of our town, told through the lens of a single, steadfast landmark.

From its earliest days as a silent-movie and vaudeville house, the Broadway Theatre immediately became a draw for the region, bringing energy, commerce and visitors to our downtown. Broadway buzzed with excitement and local businesses thrived alongside the theatre. The latter half of the 20th century brought more moviegoers, but also added country music and thousands of country music fans. I can recall standing on the sidewalk outside, catching glimpses of tour buses and knowing that a star was in town. For a small town like ours, those moments brought magic and more importantly, they brought people. Once again, the theatre drew crowds and commerce, keeping Pitman's economic engine humming. My view from inside the theatre in those years was from those plush red seats as a teenager, watching movies with friends and my future wife, popcorn in hand — moments that felt larger than life.

In 2006, when the Broadway Theatre was lovingly restored and then reopened as a live performance venue, it ushered in a renaissance for both the building and the borough. The strong sense of volunteerism in our community was evident even in those early days of the restoration and today, we welcome audiences from across the region to experience Broadway-quality shows, incredible music performances, comedians and community events. Every ticket purchased is more than just a night of entertainment — it's a step forward for our unique community, our local businesses, our sense of place and our deeply rooted civic pride.

This book is not just a chronicle of events; it's a reflection of who we are. The story of the Broadway Theatre is, in many ways, the story of Pitman itself — our resilience, our creativity and our ability to adapt, evolve and flourish through the decades.

On behalf of a grateful community, I want to offer my deepest thanks to Peter and Jill Slack and their team. Their passion, investment and stewardship of the Broadway Theatre have reignited Pitman's role as a destination, just as it was in 1926. Their vision has encouraged others to invest in Pitman and has preserved more than a building; it has preserved a legacy and given it new life for future generations to enjoy.

Here's to a century of memories as shared by our amazing storyteller Richard Eldredge and to many more acts yet to come.

Sincerely,

Michael L. Razze Jr.
Mayor of Pitman

Pitman National Bank & Trust Company

BOARDWALK SCENE, ALCYON LAKE, N. J.

Postcards from the author's collection.

1926 interior photo. Used with permission.
Athenaeum of Philadelphia.

"The opening of the
Broadway Theatre is a
fitting addition to the
business growth of Pitman
and forecasts continued
good times in business and
social activities."

The Pitman Grove Review
May 20, 1926

Screen capture from filmmaker Jason Weber's 2006, YouTube documentary on the theatre's renovation.

Bundled-up **Pitman residents walking** in the business district stopped to stare. For the first time in its 75-year history, the Pitman Broadway Theatre's marquee was eerily dark. The theatre doors, normally open for a 7 o'clock Thursday screening, were locked. Conectiv Energy had cut power to the southern New Jersey landmark after owner Daniel Munyon failed to pay a $13,500 electric bill.

At his house, Munyon was busy on the phone with a power company representative, desperately trying to work out a payment plan.

The theatre – billed as "Gloucester County's Largest Playhouse" when it debuted in 1926 – had been dark for a week and Munyon knew it had to open in 24 hours for weekend business or he was facing bankruptcy. The financial struggles of the business district's anchor attraction were echoed up and down Broadway: The furniture store on the other side of Theatre Avenue was gone. The hardware store had shuttered. Both banks on the street sat empty.

The previous spring and summer, a road-improvement project had limited traffic to the town's commercial district for months. Business at the Broadway had dropped off a cliff, from 250 weekly patrons to about 50. The theatre's roof, in need of replacing, was leaking in multiple places and plaster had begun falling from the aging structure's walls.

But by July 4, with the road project finished, Munyon's theatre regulars had returned. He was feeling more confident. In addition to screening popular second-run movies, he inked a two-year deal with a Philadelphia concert promoter to bring Patty Loveless, Arlo Guthrie, Dwight Yoakam and Gordon Lightfoot to the Broadway stage. First exposed to a classic movie house at age 8, Munyon had made it his lifelong mission to own one. Show business was in his blood, passed down from his grandmother Mary Smith Munyon, a vaudeville singer and dancer who had played the Philadelphia and South Jersey theatre circuit.

After nine years of volunteering at the Broadway and then working for owner Clayton E. Platt learning the business, Munyon bought the theatre in 1999. From the start, Munyon and business partner Charles Kern had difficulty staying ahead of the building's many ailments.

"It felt like climbing uphill backwards every day," explains Munyon.

The plight of Pitman's iconic venue had attracted the attention of the Camden Courier-Post. "There's too much history here to lose and I'm going to do my best not to let it happen," Munyon told the paper. The beleaguered business owner had every reason to feel upbeat when the article landed on the Sept. 9, 2001, front page. The story read like an invitation to reconnect with an old friend. But two days later, everyday life in the United States was halted when a terrorist attack killed 2,977 Americans and disintegrated the World Trade Center in New York.

In addition to electricity, it was costing Munyon $400 every three days for oil to heat the theatre. As he put in 15-hour workdays, Munyon dressed in layers until it was time to fire up the furnace at 5 p.m. for customers coming to the movies.

Alice Polocz, the owner of Bob's Hobbies and Crafts a few doors down the street, told a reporter she wanted to see the theatre remain a vital part of the community. "He's sort of walking a little tightrope there," she acknowledged. "Hopefully, he'll be able to hang on."

In an attempt to bolster business, the Broadway's owner was throwing anything he could at the theatre's crumbling plaster walls to see what might stick. He invited nearby Rowan University film students to screen their work. He sent shuttles to pick up seniors at the Pitman Manor on weekday afternoons and screened classics like "The Philadelphia Story" and "Casablanca." He and his wife, Mary Ann, opened a café serving coffee and desserts on the theatre's second floor.

But in the final quarter of 2002 alone, Munyon confirmed to the Courier-Post, the Broadway lost $21,000. "We're down, but we're not out," he said. "[The theatre] has got to be here for the next generation or it's a lost piece of our history."

Finally, Munyon received the call from his lawyer he had been dreading. Bankruptcy was imminent. He immediately dialed his partner Charlie Kern. "I need you to bail out," Munyon told him. "I've already put everything I own into this, so there's nothing left for them to take from me. But you're a different story." On Munyon's advice, Kern signed the paperwork dissolving their partnership.

The theatre closed and the Broadway's signature neon peacock marquee once again went dark.

An April 23, 2005, Courier-Post editorial, "Pitman Broadway Theatre Worth Saving," attempted to rally public support for the historic structure: "Pitman residents shouldn't have to look at another once-thriving business sit dark and empty. Borough officials ought to act to do what they can to help the theatre live on. With its balcony and opera-style boxes, original chandeliers, purple velvet stage curtain and restored pipe organ, the Broadway Theatre is a historical treasure."

Unfortunately, Pitman's cherished historical treasure, now under the control of a court-appointed trustee, had a looming date with a sheriff's sale.

1933 Broadway Theatre program. From the author's collection.

1906 postcard. From the author's collection.

"An Investment in the Future"
1888–1926

On the morning of April 3, 1888, the chimes of the Gloucester County Courthouse clock alerted onlookers excitedly clustered below that court proceedings were about to begin. The crowd pushed its way into the Woodbury, New Jersey, courtroom hoping to hear details of the breach of promise lawsuit being brought against Dr. Henry Harrison Carr, a young Pitman Grove physician, by his alleged former fiancé, Lulu Justice.

Henry and Lulu's private relationship had spilled into public view the previous August when Justice, 22, Carr's childhood sweetheart, filed a breach of promise suit against him, the first of its kind in Gloucester County. The titillating story instantly became front-page news in the Camden Daily Courier. Justice was seeking $10,000 from the well-liked 23-year-old doctor, who had built a growing practice in Pitman and nearby Mullica Hill. Years earlier, the friends had become romantically involved while Carr was attending Hahnemann Medical College in Philadelphia. But he later fell in love with Laura Ann Dawson and broke off the relationship with Justice. Aside from being Gloucester County's first-ever "breach of promise" suit, the requested $10,000 for damages (the equivalent of a quarter of a million dollars today) had created significant interest in the case.

Shortly after the suit was filed, a Daily Courier reporter showed up at Carr's practice in the Pitman Grove but was unable to get the doctor's side of the story. Not surprisingly, then, the newspaper's subsequent front-page story, "A Pretty Young Lady's Suit," heavily favored the petite brunette plaintiff. Woodbury attorney Robert B. Clymer, who was representing Justice, told the Courier the case centered on "a confiding woman and a heartless man." The paper went on to breathlessly report details of Henry and Lulu's courtship: "Of pleasing manners and a general favorite, his practice soon grew to large proportions and in a few years he was in receipt of a handsome income.

"But his professional success was a death blow to Miss Justice's, breaking off their engagement and acknowledging to his former love that his heart belonged to another. It was a cruel blow to his pretty sweetheart. ... Miss Justice finally consulted Lawyer Clymer who said he has strong documentary evidence showing the several promises of marriage and he expected great things from Miss Justice's testimony, as he anticipated she would certainly scorch Dr. Carr at the trial."

The smaller Bridgeton Pioneer newspaper was more circumspect in its coverage. Playing the lawsuit at the bottom of Page 5, it reported, "Justice claims she has documentary evidence of their intended marriage. Dr. Carr denies this."

Meanwhile, the Camden Daily Courier (with its larger circulation) declared, "The suit has created a social sensation in Gloucester County that has seldom been equaled." Consequently, the salacious coverage of the case attracted the attention of citizens throughout southern New Jersey. So, on the morning of April 3, 1888, it was a bit anticlimactic for the assembled when the attorneys representing the interested parties told Justice Charles G. Garrison the case had been settled amicably out of court — without revealing details of said settlement.

"It makes sense that the case made the papers, because $10,000 was a lot of money in 1888," says Dr. Carr's grandson Warren Carr, a Woodbury attorney who served as the solicitor for the Borough of Pitman for 25 years. "I heard about the case over the years from family members. The details of the settlement were never released publicly. Keep in mind, a visit to my grandfather's doctor's office back then was 50 cents."

This much is known — Henry Carr and Laura Ann Dawson had quietly gotten married on Dec. 28, 1887. "The two families, the Carrs and the Dawsons, had been close for many years," explains Warren Carr. "Dawson, my grandmother's father, was a farmer who was also a wholesale merchant on Front Street in Philadelphia. In those days, most people were introduced through church. With horse and carriage as the mode of transportation, your selection was pretty limited."

The 1888 lawsuit and settlement and its accompanying front-page headlines, had unexpected benefits. Twenty years later, by the fall of 1908, as the foundation was being poured for Henry and Laura Carr's lavish new home on

Broadway, in the center of Pitman's bustling business district, Carr was one of Gloucester County's wealthiest and best-known residents. Henry and his brother George had started both the Farmers National Bank in Mullica Hill and, later, the postcard-worthy Holmesburg-granite-constructed Pitman National Bank & Trust, which would debut in 1911 at 106 S. Broadway. The brothers were also co-owners of Alcyon Park, Pitman's popular lakeside resort attraction.

To construct their dream home, the Carrs had selected well-known building contractor William A. Lacy of Richwood. With practically every hammer blow, the Gloucester County Democrat dutifully updated readers on the structure's progress, stating, "the doctor's house promises to be the handsomest in town." When completed in the summer of 1909, the Carr property (including a stable accented with stonework to match the main house) stretched the length of a city block. "One would have to go quite a distance to find a house its equal and it reflects much credit upon the artistic sense of the doctor and the builder, Mr. Lacy," the Democrat posited. Over the years, the stable at the back of the Carr property transitioned from housing horses and carriages to the doctor's automobiles.

The three-story Carr mansion, with its distinctive wraparound porches and handsome stonework, came to symbolize Pitman's astonishing growth following the opening of the Pitman Grove in 1871. The land adjacent to a cooling lake was ideal for Methodist camp meetings held outside in South Jersey summers. The town, founded in 1905, was named in honor of Methodist minister Charles Pitman. As church camp meeting attendance swelled with each subsequent year, the 500 tents originally erected for worshippers were replaced by summer cottages. The small seasonal homes were built in a circle, with narrow streets just wide enough for pedestrians, forming a wagon-spokes formation around the camp auditorium. The 12 streets were an homage to Christ's 12 apostles.

This would become the Pitman Grove.

So sacred was the Sabbath for parishioners, a deal had been struck with the railroad that forbade the train from stopping locally on Sundays. In his 1955 book "Cottagers and Commuters: A History of Pitman, New Jersey" author and Glassboro State College history professor Dr. Harold F. Wilson wrote that visitors were required to get off either in nearby Glassboro or Sewell and walk to town on foot or take a horse and carriage. However, on Sundays those horses and carriages had to be parked outside the First Avenue main gate to the Pitman Grove, which was locked on "the Lord's day."

By 1878, Wilson writes, "six trains stopped a day in Pitman" and the town boasted nearly 300 cottages, a large general store, "four restaurants, a barber, butcher shop, a book store and an ice cream saloon." (Sales of liquor were strictly forbidden in the religious community.) By 1880, Pitman was attracting 10,000 to 12,000 people each summer and a growing influx of year-round residents, charmed by the friendly, faith-focused small town. The town's close proximity to Philadelphia (26 minutes by train) also made Pitman an attractive alternative for the City of Brotherly Love's growing workforce. By 1905, with Pitman's official formation as a borough and the election of its first mayor, Joseph M. McCowan, trains were finally permitted to stop in town on Sundays. Gas, electric and telephone utilities were also being brought on line for the town's burgeoning population.

Dr. Henry H. Carr
"The First Congressional District of New Jersey, Vol. 2." Gloucester County Historical Society.

"My grandfather decided to move his medical practice from Mullica Hill to Pitman because he always saw Pitman as a place that would grow," explains Warren Carr. "He knew any community that was serviced by the railroad had a bright future. My grandfather wanted to be a part of that." With no hospital in the vicinity, the large Carr estate on Broadway also served a practical purpose in the community. In addition to seeing patients there, Dr. Carr could perform minor surgeries on-premises and he had room for patients to stay a few days during their recovery.

In addition to his showstopping residence and practice at 39 South Broadway, Henry Carr and his brother George had attained "wide influence" in the town, assessed Wilson in "Cottagers and Commuters." Early on, George had purchased 192 acres, which in 1892 became Alcyon Lake, the sawmill and the Alcyon Park boardwalk, a popular summer attraction. Henry (who simply dropped the H from "halcyon") came up with the lake's name to reflect the body of water's peacefulness. "My grandfather Henry and his brother George operated the [Alcyon Lake] sawmill in town and Alcyon Lake provided the water power to run the mill," remembers Warren Carr. By 1912, in addition to its signature lake, the park featured a merry-go-round, bathhouse, bowling alley, steeplechase and a new Steel Pier-inspired toboggan roller coaster.

That same summer, eight miles away in Woodbury, teenager Ralph D. Wilkins began working for his father, Howard, at Green's Opera House. The performing arts centerpiece of the block-long G.G. Green Building at 108 S. Broad St. in Woodbury had been erected in 1880. It was named for benefactor George G. Green, a Civil War colonel who had made his fortune selling elixirs containing laudanum (essentially opium poppy in alcohol). As a result, Col. Green became a patent medicine king and Woodbury's first multimillionaire. In his book "South Jersey Movie Houses," author Allen Hauss explains that Green built the block-long structure to provide Gloucester's county seat with much-needed entertainment and retail space. (The building has since been named a historic landmark.)

The three-story, 1,100-seat facility's Aug. 25, 1881, grand opening featured Baker's Comic Opera Company's presentation of "Doctor of Alcantara." The evening's program informed attendees, "The new opera house is a marvel of beauty and elegance, being fitted up in every detail in Mr. Green's usual princely style — Beautiful realistic scenery, luxuriant opera chairs and gilded and colored decorations."

As the colonel's private secretary, Howard Wilkins ran the opera house's operations.

In 1912, Wilkins brought in his son Ralph, fresh out of high school, to help out. While Ralph had grown up spending hours with his father at Green's, like most young people his age, he wasn't much interested in popular opera. The younger Wilkins was more fixated on the new art form sweeping the country — moving pictures. Silent pictures had come a long way from the first public showings of the 11-minute "The Great Train Robbery," shot in 1903 on a budget of $150. By the time Ralph Wilkins had graduated from high school in 1912, the average Hollywood film was 30 minutes long and had a budget of $30,000 to $50,000 and more than 10,000 silent-movie venues (most of which were nickelodeons) had opened across the country. As Ralph Wilkins later recounted in a 1945 issue of the trade

1920s-era postcard. From the author's collection.

paper Box Office, he eventually convinced his father to "show pictures on the second floor of the opera house, one-reel subjects from Biograph, Kalem, Selig or Pathe and an illustrated song, all for five cents."

In Pitman, a year later, on Nov. 8, 1913, moving pictures came to town when the Hunt's Park Theatre, the borough's first venue dedicated exclusively to showing films, debuted on West Jersey Avenue, conveniently adjacent to Pitman's busy train station. The theatre was one of many owned and operated by New Jersey movie theatre magnate William C. Hunt, a pioneer in the business. While films had previously been shown in town, Hunt's Park became Pitman's first full-time movie theatre.

In a fall 1913 edition, the Camden Morning Post reported, "The new Park Theatre opened on Saturday night as a first-class moving picture house. The place will be open every evening except Sunday and Pitman will thus enjoy a long-felt want. Much success is predicted for the new venture." The Hunt's Park quickly became a community center. In 1914, Charles A. Reynolds, president of the Keystone Leather Company of Camden, addressed residents on "The Danger of Indecision." In 1918, Pitman Mayor Andrew J. Trucksess, the first Democrat elected to the position, presided over a patriotic rally at the theatre to mark the country's one-year anniversary of entering World War I. Three vaudeville acts also graced the Hunt's stage each Saturday night before the feature film.

Meanwhile, in Woodbury, by 1919, as author Hauss notes in "South Jersey Movie Houses," Green's Opera House had largely abandoned live performances in favor of motion pictures. At age 77, Col. Green agreed to sell the opera house to Howard Wilkins, who had formed the Woodbury Amusement Company. With his 25-year-old son Ralph's help and assistance from architects Hoffman and Henon, Wilkins converted the structure into Woodbury's "beautiful new picture house," the 1,100-seat Rialto Theatre.

In the frigid winter of 1921, in addition to seeing patients at his Pitman office, Dr. Henry Carr traveled all over South Jersey in his automobile making house calls. But in early March, Carr himself required a doctor after falling ill. On March 30, at age 57, Henry H. Carr died of pneumonia and complications from diabetes at his Broadway mansion, leaving behind his wife, Laura, daughter Evelyn and son George. The physician was buried at the Richwood Methodist Church cemetery. Carr's death would reverberate all across Pitman, from the marquee of the Hunt's Park Theatre on West Jersey Avenue down to the Alcyon Park boardwalk and end up completely transforming the town's business district.

In June, Henry's brother George W. Carr and Laura, Carr's widow, sold Alcyon Park to a pair of South Jersey investors (although George was retained as manager of the park). By the 1920s, thanks to its popularity as a Methodist summer camp and its proximity to Philadelphia, Pitman was growing by leaps and bounds. Roads were getting paved, streetlights were being installed and infrastructure improvements were made to accommodate a fast-growing population. Dr. Walter A. Rulon, the new owner of Hotel Pitman, was busy rewiring the place and added a large dining room to attract a year-round clientele and local organizations like the Rotary and Kiwanis clubs, which now regularly met at the hotel.

But in addition to the hotel enhancements, grocers and drugstores, Pitman needed an economic engine to attract more visitors and more growth. Pitman businessman Abe Applebaum and developer William Lacy's gaze fell on the centrally located Broadway mansion that Lacy had completed in 1909. They quietly approached Laura Carr about selling the estate. And in the spring of 1924, operating under the newly formed Pitman Realty Company, Applebaum arranged the sale, buying the property from Carr for $37,000.

"My grandmother was inclined to sell the big house, as she no longer needed it," says Warren Carr. "With the exception of some help, she was there all by herself. The property was subdivided and my grandmother retained the back half of the property, which contained the stable, which she turned into the new house. She did not want to leave the immediate area, so this was an ideal solution."

By 1927, a large, two-story colonial-style house retaining the stable's stonework had been built on the parcel of land at 36 Simpson Ave., directly behind where the picturesque Broadway mansion she shared with her husband had once stood. It's the same house where Laura's son, George, would raise her grandson Warren Carr.

The March 13, 1924, edition of the Camden Daily Courier broke the news that the Carr mansion would be razed to make way for "a large new theatre erected upon the site in the heart of the business section of Pitman." On Feb. 17, demolition of the beautiful property at 39 S. Broadway commenced. By the end of March, the mansion was completely gone. The Pitman Realty Company hired the Philadelphia architecture firm of Magaziner, Eberhard and Harris to design what their blueprints referred to as the "Pitman Theatre" project. The May 3, 1925, Philadelphia Inquirer reported that "the structure will be constructed of brick, cinder block, cut stone and terra cotta" and would house not only a two-story theatre, but a block of stores and apartments as well. Not surprisingly, William Lacy won the bid to one-up his previous 1909 architectural achievement on the property.

"Theatres were becoming popular, so it made good economic sense," says Warren Carr. "Almost every town had one. Applebaum, who was an attorney, Lacy and the rest of the folks who made up the Pitman Realty Company knew a theatre would be a moneymaker. It was an investment in the future. As evidenced by the things he was involved with, there isn't any question my grandfather liked progress. I think he would have been pleased."

By the fall of 1925, construction on the structure was in full swing on South Broadway. Over on West Jersey Avenue, Hunt's Park Theatre operator and projectionist Eugene Vermont "Monte" Mathis eyed the construction of the 1,200-seat, $250,000 theatre nervously.

Up in Woodbury, at the Rialto, Harold and Ralph Wilkins were also successfully leveraging the growing popularity of silent-movie houses. On Saturday nights, seats were going for 35 cents on the main floor, while the balcony cost a quarter to see the feature film along with live vaudeville acts and orchestra. But in 1925, the Wilkinses decided to cash in on their booming investment, selling the Rialto Theatre to the Stanley Company of America.

Back in Pitman, Monte Mathis was still packing them in at the Hunt's Park. Charlie Chaplin's latest hit "The Gold Rush" was billed as the "laughing success of a lifetime." By spring, locals were busily signing up for the theatre's April 6 Charleston dance contest. But as contestants bounced and flapped onstage, eager to win the cash prize being offered, the festive evening may have been the last where Monte Mathis felt like dancing. Like the musicians aboard the Titanic in 1912, Mathis could see the iceberg looming on the horizon and there was nothing he could do to get out of its path. A few hundred feet away on Pitman's main street, the hulking stone Broadway Theatre stood, nearly completed.

Inside the Pitman train station, travelers were busy gazing at the headline splashed across the April 22, 1926, edition of the Woodbury Daily Times: "New Broadway Theatre at Pitman to Open Next Month." The article, which detailed "the expressions of enthusiasm and wonder being heard daily concerning the beauty and size of Gloucester County's newest playhouse," also contained one other scoop for local residents.

To manage their new enterprise, the Pitman Realty Company had leased their new showplace to a pair of experienced movie theatre operators from Woodbury — Ralph and Howard Wilkins. The teenager who had first talked his dad into showing moving pictures at Green's Opera House in 1912 was now 32 years old and about to dedicate the rest of his life to running Pitman's Broadway Theatre.

1926 interior photo. Used with permission.
Athenaeum of Philadelphia.

CHAPTER TWO

"Meet Me at the Broadway, Gloucester County's Amusement Center"
1926–1933

The line of Pitmanites stretched down the sidewalk as the town's brand-new Broadway Theatre opened its doors for public inspection on Tuesday, May 18, 1926. William Lacy's creation extended all the way from 35 to 43 S. Broadway, the theatre's new address. Overhead were four new apartments with decorative black wrought iron balconies. Locals, along with members of the press, eagerly stepped past the three as-yet-unfinished storefronts as the Broadway, the focal point of the block-long structure, made its public debut.

After nearly a year of ignoring construction of the town's new signature theatre in its pages (perhaps in deference to the Hunt's Park, a longtime advertiser), the Pitman Grove Review finally relented with an April 29, 1926, front-page story brimming with details:

"The new Broadway Theatre is being rushed to completion by Contractor W.A. Lacy. The organ men are now on their third week installing the big three-man-

ual Kimball orchestral organ considered to be the biggest and finest instrument this side of Philadelphia. The decorators, Cibelli & Co., are applying their artistic brushes to the main floor walls, the upper floor and ceiling are being completed.

"The seating contractor has already installed all the balcony seats and the main floor chairs are being placed immediately. The beautiful crystal lighting fixtures will soon be installed; also the many changes of scenery which requires 10,000 feet of rope to operate. This scenery is now being completed in the Metropolitan Opera House, Philadelphia, by Fetters & Fisher Studios, the best of scenery artists. The big asbestos curtain weighing half a ton and measuring 40 ft. in width and 24 ft. in height is being finished and will be hung next week.

"The manager of the Broadway, Ralph D. Wilkins, 32, states that many high grade photoplays have already been contracted for. These pictures, playing Philadelphia's best class of theatres, will have first showing in this section at the Broadway."

Upon its completion, along with the Pitman National Bank and the town's churches, the Broadway Theatre immediately became one of the most admired buildings in the borough. Its ornate stonework, imposing columns and large wrought iron and milk glass sconces hung above the gleaming glass movie poster cases brought a new gravitas to the town's business district. The theatre's large vertical BROADWAY marquee, outlined in large electric bulbs, could be seen from practically anywhere on Pitman's main street. The new theatre, with its block of storefronts, along with the town's busy train station, made a statement. It informed visitors that Pitman was on the move, far removed from its quiet church camp origins. Flags were hung outside businesses all along Broadway, thanks to a board of trade letter sent out to borough shopkeepers asking them to observe May 18 as a local holiday in honor of the new theatre.

Broadway Theatre's opening night feature, May 19, 1926.
From the author's collection.

Inside, Pitmanites, accustomed to the small, simple Hunt's Park Theatre, gasped at the beautiful French Revival movie palace around them. The ornate plasterwork, crystal chandeliers, Parisian wallpaper, carpeting, red velvet stage curtains and eight luxurious boxes were unlike anything else in South Jersey. A reporter from the Gloucester County

Democrat estimated that more than 2,000 people jammed the aisles, the stage, the richly carpeted mezzanine and the balcony. All of the theatre's 1,200 seats, including the 50 box seats, were filled. While the balcony had simple wooden seats emblazoned with a B at the end of each row, patrons in the orchestra section enjoyed cushier, spring-enhanced upholstered seats.

Congratulatory floral arrangements from local businesses filled the stage. Many of the same businesses took out ads in the Pitman Grove Review to welcome the Broadway Theatre. Manager Ralph D. Wilkins told the Democrat, "The public has responded to the invitation more than my highest expectations. It is the intention of the management to respond to this display of confidence by giving the people high-grade performances."

In its coverage, the Woodbury Daily Times reported, "On the mezzanine floor is located a magnificent reception and lounge where friends may meet at their convenience prior to performances. This room has a handsome large fireplace and electronically illuminated drinking fountains with numerous beveled plate glass mirrors at every turn." The Camden Daily Courier noted that the theatre's impressive sight lines featured "a full view presented from every seat in the house." The 40-foot stage boasted a depth of 28 feet and a fly space that extended multiple stories overhead. A stairway to the right of the stage led down to four dressing rooms, a green room and restrooms for performers.

Much attention was paid to the theatre's elaborate $15,000 organ from the W.W. Kimball Company, with its 10-foot pipe chambers installed on each side of the stage.

Locals attending the public inspection got to hear the magnificent instrument for the first time. The organ's double-touch system included marimbaphones, glockenspiel, chimes, orchestra bells, harp, drums and numerous other instruments. The Pitman Grove Review reported, "In size, this organ compares favorably with those found in America's biggest cinema palaces. Organists of prominence will be heard daily in programs of high class music. The Broadway Orchestra, composed of 10 musicians, will be under the direction of O.E. Wardwell."

"The Kimball was certainly a powerful instrument," reflected John Wilkins, grandson of Ralph Wilkins, in 2006. "It could overwhelm the theatre with its volume. Many folks came to the theatre just to hear the organ." Adds the Broadway's current organist, Nathan Figlio: "Ralph Wilkins went around to all of the New York showrooms and chose the Kimball because it was the most tonally refined. It was also the most expensive but the best-built. The proof of that is we do very little to it even now and it works day in and day out."

In its inaugural newspaper ads, the Broadway called attention to its ventilation system, touting its "latest design with a complete change of air every minute." The theatre's state-of-the-art air circulation system was a result of America's "Fresh Air Movement," which originated in the aftermath of the deadly Spanish flu epidemic of 1918-1920 in an era when influenza and tuberculosis were among the deadliest illnesses in the country. Like the global Covid pandemic a century later, the airborne diseases could sicken people lingering inside spaces with poor air circulation.

The theatre's elaborate lighting system, anchored by two gorgeous crystal chandeliers in the main auditorium plus a third in the lobby, was also a source of wonder for attendees. Reported the Grove Review: "Three circuits in the fixtures, providing red, blue and amber colors, offer a multitude of harmonious color blending effects. The two main ceiling fixtures, in particular, are composed of imported crystals, measuring eight feet in length and each is a thing of beauty." Remarkably, these chandeliers and signature-colored lighting remain a feature at each Broadway live performance a century later.

Many of the same locals returned the following evening, May 19, for shows at 6:30 and 9 p.m., featuring high-class vaudeville acts, the Broadway Orchestra and a feature film, the just-released Paramount Pictures silent comedy "The New Klondike." Orchestra seats were 50 cents, while a balcony seat could be obtained for 35 cents.

Theatre manager Ralph Wilkins had hired an all-female usher team of high school students, instantly identifiable by their rose-colored linen dresses with white collars, to hand out programs, take tickets and guide patrons to their seats. The inaugural Broadway Theatre usher team included 15-year-old Pitmanite Sally Titus. "Mr. Wilkins told me, 'If anyone asks, you're 16,'" recalled Sally Titus-Cline to Gloucester County Times columnist Bob Shryock 62 years later with a laugh. "The jobs weren't easy to come by. Many girls applied and as soon as somebody left there would be others waiting to replace them. It was a wonderful way to make $4 a week. I saved my money to buy the clothes I needed to go on the senior class trip to Washington D.C."

Photo courtesy of Brandon Hedenberg.
Hedenberg Real Estate Company.

After working the mobbed opening night, Titus expected to be off the following evening, but Wilkins called her into work because the theatre was once again at capacity. Of Ralph Wilkins, she recalled, "He was a quiet man and a nice boss who treated us lovely. We averaged 75 cents a night, which in those days came in handy. We were so busy we'd see the same movie three or four times in the two nights it played and never really had a chance to look at it."

In the 1988 interview Titus-Cline also remembered: "It's still a beautiful theatre. It's very nostalgic for me. But then I smell the popcorn and it takes it all away." The Broadway's signature lobby concession stand — and sales of hot buttered popcorn — were added later on. A vending machine sold candy for a nickel to the theatre's early patrons. After their shifts, Titus and the other teenage ushers would meet down the street at the Dilks' Drug Store soda fountain for their preferred beverage, Tak-Aboost, a carbonated citrus drink, served with a pretzel dangling from the straw.

Hunt's Park projectionist Monte Mathis. Photo courtesy of Pitman Historical Museum.

Up on West Jersey Avenue at the Hunt's Park Theatre, manager and projectionist Monte Mathis saw the lines snaking down Broadway outside "Gloucester County's Largest Playhouse" (as Ralph Wilkins was billing it in the theatre's half-page Pitman Grove Review ad) and knew the fight for his survival was on. Earlier in the month, he had helped bolster the smaller theatre's bottom line by booking the Lon Chaney thriller "Phantom of the Opera." In addition to a fresh coat of paint, the owner and South Jersey theatre magnate William C. Hunt had authorized other alterations, including rearranging the seats and adding "decorations on the ceiling and walls."

As the annual Pitman Grove Methodist camp attendees began arriving in the summer of 1926, Ralph and Howard Wilkins were committed to making a solid first impression on potential new customers. Onscreen in the Broadway's opening months were silent film queen Clara Bow in "The Runaway," W.C. Fields in "It's the Old Army Game" and

Gloria Swanson in "The Untamed Lady," plus exclusive live concerts, including The Women's Symphony Orchestra of Philadelphia. On July 26 and 27, the Wilkinses loaned the theatre out to the Pitman Athletic Association to present Zane Grey's "Born to the West" as a fundraiser for the town's amateur athletics fund.

To counter its new competition, beginning with the July 29 edition of the Pitman Grove Review, the Hunt's Park Theatre began an aggressive advertising campaign. The venue began taking out ads on the page opposite the Broadway Theatre's. The Broadway ad promised readers: "Foremost photoplay entertainment and refined surroundings. This theatre has a most modern ventilating system, 4 great acts of vaudeville plus the Broadway Orchestra, 35 and 50 cents." Lacking those amenities, the Hunt's Park promised patrons a bargain: "The House With The Best Pictures. Don't forget that we are giving you the very finest pictures that money can buy. All at 10 cents for everybody. When you see better photoplays, it will be at Hunt's Park Theatre, Pitman, NJ." The Broadway countered by booking "Byrd's American Polar Triumph," the latest footage of Arctic explorer Robert Byrd's travels.

By August, the Broadway Theatre was referring to itself in its ads as "Gloucester County's Amusement Center, where new friends are becoming steady patrons." On the opposite page, the Hunt's Park ad boasted: "Bang!! Bang!! Another Broken Record Just TRY to beat this line-up at 10 cents everybody." But the Broadway had saved its most tantalizing promotion for the bottom of its ad: "Special Announcement: On Saturday afternoon, the management of this theatre has engaged a motion picture camera man to go about Pitman taking scenes of interest and all those who want to be photographed. See yourself on the screen of the Broadway, week of Aug. 16. Various organizations, fire companies, etc. will be photographed, including the bathing beauties at Alcyon Lake."

In September, the Hunt's Park Theatre managed to snag silent film heartthrob Rudolph Valentino's swan song, "The Son of the Sheik," with this note to patrons: "By special arrangement, the management has secured camera portraits of the late star, which will be given to any who wish them." But by November, the Hunt's Park's bargain-basement pricing had begun to wobble – admission on the slow nights of Monday and Tuesday remained 10 cents but increased to 15 and 20 cents the rest of the week. The Broadway, meanwhile, hosted all-day screenings plus vaudeville on Thanksgiving and Christmas Day.

Robert Gowen, the Broadway's first organist. Used with permission. Gloucester County Historical Society.

In just seven months, Pitman's Broadway Theatre had grown so successful, the theatre's contractor and Pitman Realty Company president, W.A. Lacy and its operators, Ralph and Howard Wilkins, joined financial forces to buy the Broadway outright. As the Pitman Grove Review had predicted that spring, "The opening of the Broadway [is] an event that will long be remembered as a milestone in the growth of Pitman's business and social life." Hoping to capitalize on the theatre's momentum, new homes on Pitman's Linden Avenue were being advertised in the Camden Courier for $6,500 with $500 down.

As intended, the Broadway had brought a boom to the town's commercial district and inspired new businesses to open. In its grand-opening ad, the new Holly Inn touted, "Home cooking the same as mother's." A ham or roast beef dinner with mashed potatoes, scalloped tomatoes, coleslaw, hot rolls and choice of pie, ice cream or pudding could be enjoyed for 65 cents. By mid-1927, the town's theatre war was over. After 14 years, the marquee at the Hunt's Park Theatre on West Jersey Avenue, Pitman's first movie house, was dimmed forever. The prime real estate space next to the train station would soon become a bowling alley. Hunt's Park projectionist Monte Mathis' expertise would be valued for the next 38 years in nearby Vineland, first at the Grand Theatre and, later, at the new Landis Theatre, where he would oversee film projection until his death in 1965.

While Pitman was certainly amenable to embracing the future (by 1905, trains were stopping at the Pitman station on the Sabbath), the borough council and residents still drew certain societal lines in the sand. While you could pay 35 cents to see vaudeville, shorts like "Flaming Flappers" and the new W.C. Fields comedy "So's Your Old Man" at the Broadway, borough council promptly voted down proposed professional boxing matches in town. But for entertainment enthusiasts, not all the news coming out of the council meetings was negative. The council approved the widening of Broadway between Pitman and Theatre avenues to help lessen traffic congestion. Estimated cost: $1,800.

Given the Broadway Theatre's immediate popularity, the Wilkinses and W.A. Lacy were able to secure bigger titles for patrons, like MGM's lavish hit "The Big Parade." The two-and-a-half-hour World War I epic raked in $3.4 million for the studio. But the Broadway faced a fresh challenge when its owners wanted to book the new Fox romantic drama "7th Heaven," starring Janet Gaynor and Charles Farrell, for Valentine's Day week in 1928. The film (which would net Gaynor the Best Actress Oscar at the inaugural Academy Awards in 1929) featured synchronized sound. While the war-set romance remained a standard silent film with dialogue cards, it also boasted a synchronized musical score and sound effects achieved with the new Movietone sound system.

In less than two years, the Broadway, originally envisioned in 1925 as a state-of-the-art silent-movie house, was already being rendered obsolete by emerging technology. But by the time MGM's first sound picture "Alias Jimmy Valentine," with William Haines and Lionel Barrymore, was released, Ralph Wilkins had come up with a solution. As author Harold Wilson noted in "Cottagers and Commuters," the Broadway Theatre had now installed all-new sound equipment "at great expense," and the theatre could present "all the best in synchronized and talk pictures." "7th Heaven" finally hit the screen at the Broadway the same month Hollywood released Al Jolson's groundbreaking "The Jazz Singer," the first feature-length film with audible dialogue and musical performances.

As the Broadway became Pitman's largest community gathering space, Ralph Wilkins tried his hand at booking less conventional programs on the theatre's stage. Decades before James Beard and Julia Child taught TV viewers how to cook, Wilkins, in partnership with the Atlantic City Electric Company and HotPoint electric ranges, brought Chicago home economist Mildred Rees to Pitman for an afternoon "Electric Cooking Party." As the Pitman Grove Review described it, "The party will afford women of this community the opportunity to receive domestic science suggestions from an expert home economist as well as the opportunity of viewing electric cooking equipment in action."

Adding to the novelty of the event? While dinner cooked in the oven onstage and the smell of roasting chicken perfumed the air, Pitman housewives were treated to a screening of actor John Gilbert (known to silent film era audiences as "The Great Lover") in the 60-minute romantic drama "St. Elmo." Oh and one lucky attendee didn't have to cook that evening. The finished chicken dinner was given out to the attendee holding the matinee's lucky number. The free event was packed.

The competition between the Rialto – the Wilkinses' former movie house in Woodbury – and the Broadway remained fierce. Both were vying to screen MGM's two-and-a-half-hour, $3.9 million spectacle "Ben Hur" starring Ramon Novarro and a cast of 150,000. Two-strip Technicolor was used for nine of the film's sequences, including the birth of Christ scene. After playing long runs in major cities, the epic finally found its way across the Delaware River in April 1928. It opened on the same day in Woodbury and Pitman, but Wilkins managed to wrangle an extra day for his run. Orchestra seats cost 50 cents and the balcony was 35 cents. "This mighty spectacular picture will burn its way into your memory to last forever!" promised the Broadway newspaper ad. At the bottom, Wilkins warned would-be stragglers, "To fully enjoy it, see it from the beginning!"

Given the Broadway's success and the rising prominence of its owners, by the time the theatre celebrated its second anniversary in the spring of 1928, the Woodbury Daily Times' "Pitman Pointers" society column was routinely reporting on the afternoon teas and bridge gatherings of Ralph Wilkins' wife, Elizabeth, as well as the couple's summer vacation to Niagara Falls. The column also disclosed, "William Lacy and Ralph Wilkins, the popular owners and managers of the Broadway Theatre, have been spending a few days in New York City on business."

Back in Pitman, even without the boss, the Broadway was in more than capable hands. In August 1928, Ralph Wilkins had hired the Strand Theatre's young projectionist away from his job in nearby Clayton. Al Beckett would remain a fixture at the Broadway for the next 50 years. He had started his career at age 12, hand-cranking films at Clayton's Spectatorium in 1919. His first assignment in the projection booth at the Broadway was screening "The Patent Leather Kid," starring Richard Barthelmess as a young boxer balancing his professional and romantic life as World War I looms. On the wall in the booth, Beckett began chronicling Broadway milestones in ink. Near the end of his half-century tenure at the theatre in 1974, Beckett told Cy Eastlack for his "Cy Cez" Gloucester County Daily Times column, he was attracted to working at the Broadway because of its state-of-the-art Kim-

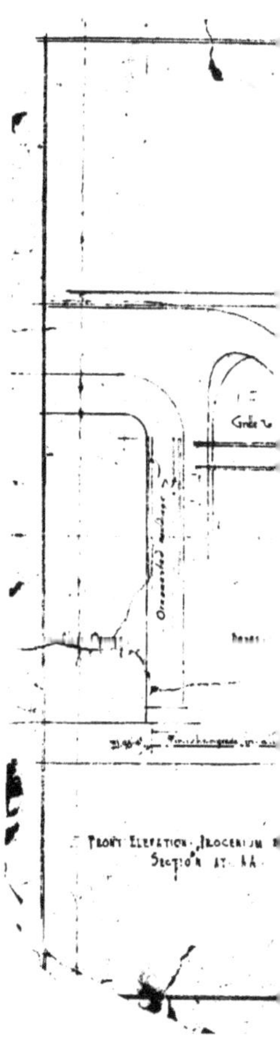

ball organ (most competing silent-movie houses relied on house pianists to play the live score to the pictures on-screen).

The Broadway Theatre's balcony, meanwhile, was becoming more popular with the town's young people as Pitman police cracked down on other venues for public displays of affection. In September 1928, the Camden Evening Courier reported, under the headline "Pitman Petters Dodge Eyes of Snooping Cops," that the town's "Lovers'

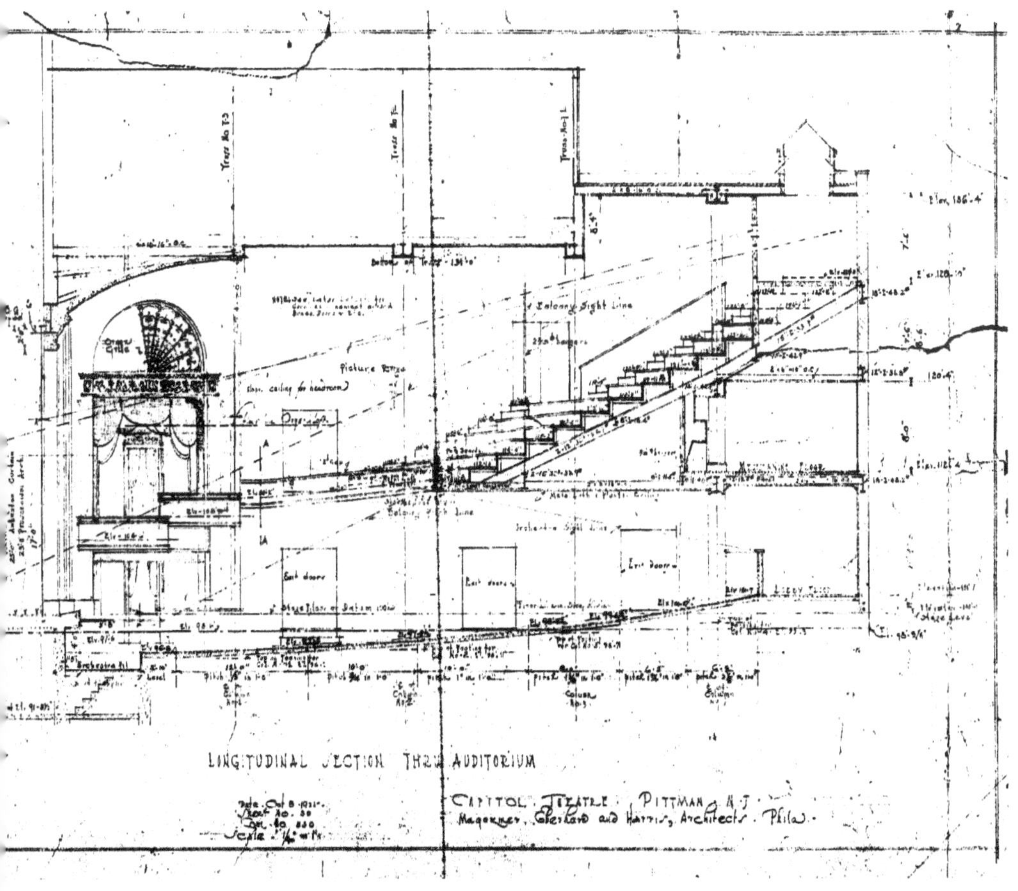

Architectural drawings for the balcony. Used with permission. Athenaeum of Philadelphia.

Lane" incidents had decreased from 271 in August to just 26. Pitman's Director of Public Safety Harold C. Nichols praised police, saying, "Some of the other towns are also going after this thing and are cleaning out their 'Lovers' Lanes.' I believe I am right in warning parents of this practice and trying to make our streets safe for our young people. There has been lots of criticism but the results have been effective."

In November 1931, to shore up a steady flow of "talkies" to the Broadway, Wilkins struck a deal with regional reps for MGM to screen Hollywood's biggest movie studio's entire slate of all-sound pictures right after they played at Keith's Theatre in Philadelphia. Wilkins was now bringing MGM's cavalcade of stars to Pitman, including Clark Gable, Greta Garbo, Norma Shearer, Joan Crawford, Ramon Novarro, William Haines and Marie Dressler, plus MGM's short subjects, including Laurel and Hardy and the "Our Gang" comedies popular with youngsters. To announce the deal, Wilkins took out quarter-page ads with headshots of MGM stars and the headline "We've Captured A Lion!" At the bottom was the theatre's new tagline, "Meet Me at the Broadway, Gloucester County's Amusement Center."

A front-page Pitman Grove Review story, disguised as a letter between two PTA-attending mothers, praised Wilkins' family-friendly film bookings at the Broadway in an era when film violence had begun sweeping the nation. Perhaps not coincidentally, the same week the Rialto was running "Frankenstein" five times a day to brisk crowds, "Ethel" wrote to "Jean" to publicly thank Wilkins. "Our moving picture manager has had to pay out of his own pocket, because he didn't think some movies were fit to be shown on our screen. He's absolutely tabooed the run of gangster films flooding the country and recently refused to show a film which is being shown in nearby towns be-

Broadway program, 1932. From the author's collection.

cause he considered it too horrible for the general public to see. Now you know, Ethel, when it hits a man's pocketbook like that, he really cares." The article/ad then goes on to promote a screening of "Sooky," starring kid actor Jackie Cooper.

While neither of the town's banks failed during the Depression, when the neighboring Glassboro Title and Trust shuttered, it gave many Pitmanites pause. In "Cottagers and Commuters," historian Harold Wilson reports that by November 1931, 54 Pitman families (about 200 total dependents) required help in some form. That same month, the nation was getting financial assistance from moviegoers. The Broadway, along with other Gloucester County movie houses, teamed up to host benefits for the Unemployed Relief Fund.

Even during the Depression, folks were still going to the movies. One huge draw for Pitmanites was the June 1932 film debut of local boy Preston Foster, reprising his New York Broadway stage role as a riveter in director Mervyn LeRoy's "Two Seconds," co-starring Edward G. Robinson. Foster was so good in the film, Warner Bros. offered him a long-term contract. Likewise, Foster's hometown movie house was growing so successful, it was inspiring competition. In Glassboro, the United Amusement Company purchased a tract of land on High Street to erect the Roxy Theatre, a 750-seat venue for silent pictures, with a stage for vaudeville acts and a Page organ. But by the time the theatre's name was changed to the Glassboro Theatre, it had a new owner — Ralph Wilkins. In a savvy business move, Wilkins was now poised to use the larger Broadway as a feeder theatre and leverage his deal with MGM to bring early "talkies" to the Glassboro the week after they played in Pitman.

While Ralph Wilkins could outmaneuver competing theatre rivals and wrangle deals with Hollywood studios, there was no preparation for the phone call he received on Oct. 28, 1933. William A. Lacy, his co-owner and friend and the contractor who'd dreamed up and then built the Broadway Theatre, was dead. Lacy, 70, was among the four fatalities when a truck collided with his car in nearby Pittsgrove.

With his father, Howard, advancing in age and Lacy's death, Ralph Wilkins was now left to run the day-to-day operations of two movie theatres alone.

"WE'VE CAPTURED A LION!"

LEO the M-G-M LION BRINGS THE STARS TO YOU!

With pride we announce that this theatre will show in the coming season the bright STARS and great entertainments of

METRO-GOLDWYN-MAYER PICTURES

A feather in our cap! Certainly, we're proud and you'll be glad! Against the keenest competition we have obtained for our patrons the most desired of all screen entertainments—Metro-Goldwyn-Mayer Pictures. Leadership in the film world has been won by M-G-M and its Stars! It is our privilege to invite you to enjoy these wonder shows in coming months at this theatre.

MARION DAVIES

GRETA GARBO

NORMA SHEARER

WALLACE BEERY

JOHN GILBERT

WILLIAM HAINES

ROBERT MONTGOMERY

JOAN CRAWFORD

RAMON NOVARRO

MARIE DRESSLER

BUSTER KEATON

LAWRENCE TIBBETT

The BROADWAY THEATRE in PITMAN

Now Becomes The
THEATRE OF THE STARS

THIS WEEK — A Big Attraction Every Day!

Starting Today with
"THE SQUAW MAN"—Cecil DeMille's big hit--with Warner Baxter

CLARK GABLE

LAUREL HARDY

Alfred LUNT & Lynn FONTANNE

Tuesday, November 24th
"SKYLINE"
with
THOMAS MEIGHAN

Wednesday, November 25th
1—BIG ACTS VAUDEVILLE—1
"CAUGHT"
Starring
Richard Arlen · Louise Dresser

Thursday, Nov. 26th, Thanksgiving Day
4—BIG ACTS VAUDEVILLE—4
JOHN GILBERT
at his best in
"The Phantom of Paris"

Friday, November 27th
JOAN CRAWFORD in
"THIS MODERN AGE"

Saturday, November 28th
4 — GREAT ACTS VAUDEVILLE — 4
ANN HARDING in "DEVOTION"
The Star of Stars in a Startling Story!

M-G-M SHORT SUBJECTS
Joy Spots on Forthcoming Programs

HAL ROACH COMEDIES—LAUREL & HARDY—CHARLIE CHASE—THE BOY FRIENDS—OUR GANG—Thelma TODD & Zasu PITTS—M-G-M's DOGVILLE COMEDIES—SPORT CHAMPIONS—FISHERMAN'S PARADISE—FLIP the FROG Cartoons—Fitzpatrick TRAVELTALKS—SIR HARRY LAUDER—HEARST METROTONE NEWS, The Globe Trotter.

Meet me at the Broadway
Gloucester County's Amusement Center

Photo courtesy of Pitman Historical Museum.

CHAPTER THREE

"An Important Announcement of Unusual Interest"
1935–1941

The scent of roasting pineapple and coconut greeted attendees arriving at the Broadway on the afternoon of March 13, 1935. The theatre was near capacity as women from across South Jersey excitedly gathered to take in the newest attraction.

Vera A. Schneider wasn't a film or vaudeville star. She was the "household efficiency expert" hired by the theatre, the Pitman Grove Review and Atlantic City Electric to host a three-afternoon cooking school live onstage with a new state-of-the-art electric stove. For her inaugural afternoon menu, Schneider demonstrated to South Jersey housewives how to prepare a dinner of Virginia-style baked ham, shredded string beans, potato balls, banana cake and, yes, pineapple "steaks" (slices of canned pineapple dipped in butter and shredded coconut and baked in a 375-degree oven for 8 to 10 minutes). Admission was free.

A year later, the annual cooking school series had proven so popular, recipe books were printed for attendees, thanks to the series sponsors, including Campbell's Soup Company, Abbott's Dairies, General Electric, McCormick & Co., W.K. Kellogg and local businesses like C.M. Kandle, White Star Laundry and Merritt's House of Flowers. The classes, held on three consecutive afternoons, were arranged thematically, with sessions dedicated to "Cookery Short Cuts," "When Company Comes" and "Old-Fashioned Bake Day." The local gas company was soon hosting its own cooking series at the theatre.

By 1938, the Pitman Grove Review Cooking School was breaking attendance records, with over 4,000 women, representing 80 nearby towns, attending the sessions. As entrées baked in the oven onstage, Sockwell's Dress Shop from nearby Clayton hosted an afternoon fashion show while M.L. Gebhard, the proprietor of Pitman's Gebhard Beauty Salon, demonstrated the latest hairstyles on six local models.

The Grove Review was raking in the advertising dollars as local businesses began professionally aligning themselves with Schneider. Garrison & Lawrence at 126 S. Broadway ran a photo of Schneider with the tagline: "Our store is her headquarters for fresh fruits, vegetables and clams to be used at the cooking school!" The Beckman butcher shop at 52 S. Broadway was busy advertising sugar-cured ham for 17 cents a pound, two dozen eggs for 55 cents and ground beef ("pure beef not suet!") for 23 cents a pound.

While local businesses, the theatre and utility companies were all reaping the rewards of the successful cooking school, one chief demographic in Pitman was ready to picket — hungry husbands. On the final day of the 1938 cooking school, Pitman Grove Review contributor Len Eckman lamented: "Dear Husbands: Did you come home expecting to have dinner steaming hot, ready on the table for you and then found out to your sorrow that you had to take leftovers instead — all because your dear wife had been out all afternoon to the Review Cooking School? If you have had this trouble, just write it down in your little black book for some future reference, for there are a great many other husbands in the same predicament."

The success of the cooking school also helped offset the film-industry-related furor Broadway owner Ralph Wilkins was encountering. As the owner of successful theatres in Pitman and Glassboro, Wilkins was elected in 1934 to a three-year term as director of the Allied Theatre Owners of New Jersey. At the organization's annual convention in Atlantic City, 200 of the state's small-town movie theatre owners gathered to demand a "return to clean movies." While the Hollywood Motion Picture Production Code (known as the Hays Code) had been adopted in 1930, it was not rigorously enforced until 1934, finally bowing to growing public pressure. In a Woodbury Daily Times front-page story, Allied President Sidney E. Samuelson lamented, "Our theatres are supported by the backbone of America. Immoral films mean poor business for us."

While Wilkins had screened MGM's precode box office hit "The Thin Man," starring the martini-swilling married detective team Nick and Nora Charles, William Powell and Myrna Loy's tamer third screen pairing, the courtroom melodrama "Evelyn Prentice," was playing when the theatre hosted a capacity-crowd of children on the morning of Jan. 19, 1935. The main attraction: a personal appearance by

Philadelphia radio star Uncle Wip. In the 1930s and early '40s, Uncle Wip was a popular children's host on 610-AM WIP whose nightly radio adventures enthralled Delaware Valley children back when the station broadcast from Gimbels Department Store in Philadelphia. A souvenir photo of Uncle Wip surrounded by children clustered under the Broadway's beautiful new neon peacock marquee was subsequently published in newspapers across South Jersey.

On May 29, 1935, the Borough of Pitman was rocked by the sudden death of George W. Carr at age 79. The brother of Dr. Henry H. Carr, longtime owner of Alcyon Park and president of Pitman National Bank, had suffered a stroke. Along with his brother, Carr had been one of the town's most beloved leaders and chief architects of Pitman's growth. Less than two years later, Ralph Wilkins would also mourn the loss at age 71 of his father, Howard, his Broadway Theatre partner and the family patriarch, who first introduced Ralph to the theatre business in 1912. Employees of the Broadway served as Wilkins' pallbearers.

Howard Wilkins would no doubt have been proud of the successful theatre proprietor Ralph had become. The younger Wilkins had an innate talent for finding unique crowd-pleasing vaudeville attractions. In December 1937, on a bill with the Bette Davis-Henry Fonda picture "That Certain Woman," Wilkins had booked Rose's Parisian Midget Follies, starring a company of "amazingly talented singing and dancing little people." Or as the Pitman Grove Review Broadway ad declared: "The Only Midget Swing Band In Existence! A thrill for the young and old." Later in the month, the Royal Mounted Police appeared live on the Broadway stage — complete with their horses, plus sled dogs Kazan and Diana starring in "Arctic Varieties," which promised to be "educational, mirthful, musical and melodious."

In 1931, as part of the Broadway's "talkies" distribution deal with MGM, the studio had helped Wilkins usher in the Broadway's era of animal acts on its stage. While on a publicity tour of theatres screening its film lineup, MGM sent a replica of its famous mascot, a caged lion named Leo, to dazzle audiences during two days of appearances at the Broadway. "See Leo perform under the direction of his trainer, Capt. Volney Ohifer," touted the Broadway's ad. The climax of Leo's stage show occurred when little Eloise Page, a tyke dressed in a lion tamer outfit, bravely entered the lion's cage to gasps from the audience.

Warren Carr, the grandson of Dr. Henry and Laura Carr, remembers such evenings well as a kid growing up behind the Broadway. "Since the theatre was designed for vaudeville, frequently we would have lions, tigers, small elephants, monkeys and all sorts of other critters on our property. There was no other place to put them."

Thanks to its ideal position between Philadelphia, Atlantic City and New York City, Pitman's Broadway Theatre was a favorite stop on the vaudeville circuit. Broadway projectionist Al Beckett began keeping track of the famous names gracing the stage, scribbling them on the wall of the projection booth. From his perch behind the spotlight, Beckett got to observe performers Bing Crosby, Bob Hope, Jimmy Durante, Red Skelton, Milton Berle, Fatty Arbuckle, Jackie Gleason, George Burns and Gracie Allen, the Andrews Sisters, Betty Hutton, Eddie Fisher and radio stars Abbott and Costello, just before they set out for Hollywood to film their first picture together. "Lou Costello was one of the nicest fellows you'd ever want to meet," Beckett later recounted to the Gloucester County Times. "People used to line up clear back to the railroad [on Pitman Avenue] to see vaudeville, even after the talkies came out. [The performers] were on their way up and we were about half-way." A wall in the downstairs dressing room soon became filled with the autographs of the rising stars.

George Burns was among the acts "half-way" to stardom when he and Allen played the Broadway. In 1992, at age 96, Burns explained the importance of playing small-town theatres in developing his act. "Today, there's no place for an entertainer to be bad. The kids have it rough. When I was starting out in vaudeville, there were places you could flop and nobody cared. In the places that were bad, I was good. The places that were good, I was bad. I played Atlantic City for the first time in 1917. They must have liked me because they just booked me again."

In addition to projecting movies, Beckett was in charge of keeping the spotlight trained on the live performers — even when things went awry on the stage below. "One time, an acrobat came down hard on the edge of the trampoline instead of the center," Beckett recalled. "His teeth went in all directions, with blood spurting all over. He put his hand over his mouth and bowed to the audience. Next show, there he was out in front of the audience. He had gone to a dentist between shows and gotten fixed up."

In February 1938, Pitmanites piled into the Broadway to see the "official pictures" of the recent Jim Braddock-Tommy Farr heavyweight championship fight at Madison Square Garden. The fight films were on a double bill with local boy Preston Foster's next big Hollywood film, "First

Lady," a D.C.-set political comedy co-starring Kay Francis. In Hollywood, Foster (or "Pidge," his boyhood nickname, as Pitmanites referred to him) was on a roll. In November, the Broadway screened his next feature, "Army Girl," a movie that made front-page news in the Pitman Grove Review when Foster's sister, Mrs. E.H. Bauzenberger Jr., who lived locally on Harding Court, visited the set. "Army Girl" was on a double bill with motion pictures shot at the recent Pitman-Glassboro high school football matchup.

Young people were also coming to see the MGM picture "Thoroughbreds Don't Cry," starring a new teen performer named Judy Garland. Her screen partner was a former Broadway Theatre vaudeville act, Joe Yule Jr. While kick-starting his film career, Yule opted to rebrand himself as Mickey Rooney. Ralph Wilkins had also scored a booking of "The Goldwyn Follies," the first MGM Technicolor film, featuring appearances by the Ritz Brothers and Edgar Bergen and Charlie McCarthy. Before setting off to Hollywood to make that picture, Bergen and his wisecracking wooden co-star had entertained the Broadway's Saturday-night vaudeville crowd in person. In the audience, sitting with his grandmother Mary that night, delighted at seeing the popular radio stars live, was 7-year-old Clayton Platt, a local kid who had been coming to shows at the Broadway since 1935. The boy was the grandson of former Pitman Mayor Andrew Trucksess, who had been elected in 1917.

The Broadway Theatre's owner always kept an eye on his chief competitor, the Rialto Theatre in Woodbury. By 1935, the Rialto had become the first movie house in South Jersey to install air conditioning. Or as their ads now proclaimed: "Air Conditioning — Cool and Comfortable." Ever the astute businessman, Ralph Wilkins picked up the phone and began making calls to his fellow Pitman Business Men's Association brethren.

While Wilkins wasn't in the habit of planting blind newspaper items to solicit press attention, in the spring of 1938 he made an exception. The April 25 edition of the Woodbury Daily Times teased readers, "Ralph Wilkins, manager of the Broadway Theatre, Pitman, will have an important announcement to make within the next few days, he intimated today. It was understood that it would be of unusual interest to theatre patrons throughout this entire section."

June 10, 1938. Gloucester County Historical Society.

The "important announcement of unusual interest" turned out to be a $10,000 state-of-the-art General Electric air-conditioning system. In its June 10, 1938, edition, the Pitman Grove Review gave the story front-page attention just under the paper's masthead: "Broadway Theatre Cooling System Now In Operation." What followed was a painstakingly detailed account of the costly and complicated installation. For starters, a 200-foot-deep well had to be dug on Theatre Avenue, which then every hour pumped

8,000 gallons of 55-degree water up to the roof, where a water "penthouse" then distributed the water through cooling coils, producing 30 tons of refrigeration.

To commemorate the occasion, the Broadway took out an igloo-accented full-page ad with a note from Ralph Wilkins promising, "Even on the hottest, stickiest days you can enjoy summer resort weather in The Broadway Theatre while you are being entertained by the screen's greatest stars."

The air conditioning's automatic, electric-thermostat-controlled system "was placed outside to avoid any noise." Well, unless you were a member of the Carr family living behind the theatre. "You could definitely hear that massive air-conditioning system running from our house behind the theatre," remembers Warren Carr with a laugh. "Before air conditioning, I remember the doors always being open to air the place out. But gradually, people wanted more and more comfort when they went to the theatre."

In the summer of 1938, Ralph Wilkins pulled out all the stops to showcase the theatre's new $10,000 amenity by booking the best new pictures for Grove summer camp visitors. As temperatures soared outside, Pitmanites sat in the air-cooled theatre to see Dorothy Lamour's new Technicolor adventure picture "Her Jungle Love." But Wilkins wasn't just skating on the Broadway's chilly new interior to bring in customers. In July, he booked the Technicolor hit "The Adventures of Robin Hood" with Errol Flynn, "the finest adventure film of the year."

Even when the G.E. air-conditioning system was snapped off for the season, Ralph Wilkins was determined to finish the year strong at the Broadway. For the holiday season, he had booked director Frank Capra's latest hit "You Can't Take It With You," with James Stewart and Jean Arthur and Shirley Temple's latest, "Just Around the Corner." Thanks to the Kiwanis Club, the children of Pitman were treated to a free screening of "Young Doctor Kildare." Moviegoers also turned out for the Mickey Rooney-Wallace Beery picture "Stablemates."

And more than a few young Pitmanites rushed through their turkey dinner to get down to the Broadway for its all-day Thanksgiving stage show. Wilkins had booked a stage full of talent winners touring in the "Major Bowes' Amateur Hour" show. The "American Idol" of its era in the 1930s and '40s, the phenomenally popular weekly NBC radio show was hosted by Major Edward Bowes. Among his discoveries: future opera star Beverly Sills, comedian Jack Carter and a skinny New Jersey kid who was then performing with his pals in the Hoboken Four, Frank Sinatra.

Behind the Broadway, over on Simpson Avenue, the mood was less festive. On November 29, Laura Dawson Carr, wife of the late Dr. Henry H. Carr, died at her home at age 72 after a lengthy illness. "I was only 3 at the time," recalls Warren Carr. "My grandparents had a very strong relationship. She never wanted to be far away from where they lived together. I learned from my parents that she was very community-minded. She truly loved Pitman and hearing the stories over the years, I learned the town loved her as well."

By the fall of 1939, just six weeks after its Hollywood premiere, Wilkins had snagged for the Broadway screen the biggest MGM release of the year — the Technicolor marvel "The Wizard of Oz," starring Judy Garland. As the Woodbury Daily Times ad touted, "At Last! The picture Hollywood always dreamed of ... in Technicolor." The film proved so popular, Ralph Wilkins even canceled the regularly scheduled Saturday-evening vaudeville.

As business boomed on Broadway, thanks to a growing population and the attractions being booked at its popular theatre, Pitman was now facing a challenge that would perplex town officials for the next 80 years — parking. Or more specifically, a lack thereof. In the fall of 1939, Ralph Wilkins was determined to address the issue and announced his candidacy for borough council. He won the seat and by spring 1940, the mayor, council and the Pitman Business Men's Association had created a special committee "to consider the establishing of a new parking area for shoppers and theatregoers" headed up by Wilkins.

In between his new duties as Pitman councilman, the Broadway's owner made time to wrangle a two-day engagement for the biggest movie of the year. And while he didn't often resort to reserved seating, MGM's four-hour Technicolor epic "Gone With the Wind" was worth

1940 Pitman Grove Review ad. Gloucester County Historical Society.

the effort. The Broadway Theatre newspaper ad said it all: "An Unforgettable Thrill." While he could only squeeze one showing of the Civil War saga in per night at 7:45 (charging the princely sum of $1.10 a seat), Wilkins ran a 1:30 p.m. screening at a discounted 75 cents. Raved The Philadelphia Inquirer: "Every film-goer had better count right now upon devoting four hours of his life to seeing [producer] David O. Selznick's picture. 'Gone With the Wind' is an honest, gorgeously effective film with enough dramatic meat to satisfy the most voracious appetite."

By Memorial Day, parking negotiations had screeched to a halt. While an area adjacent to Broadway had been identified for use, 46 Pitman business owners were now balking at having to pay for it. There was also opposition from the Pitman Grove Camp Meeting Association to "using any part of the camp meeting grove for the proposed parking area." Meanwhile, local merchants were urging council officials to extend the current parking limit from one to two hours for shoppers.

But by the time Christmas shoppers descended on Broadway for the 1940 holiday season, Wilkins had secured a deed to widen the entrance to a plot of land at Montgomery and Holly avenues. This would become downtown's much-needed new parking lot. To further entice evening shoppers, five "500 candlepower" lights had been installed in the new parking lot. Thanks to a nearly year-long effort from Wilkins, business merchants and borough council, Pitman's parking woes were in the rearview mirror — at least for the moment.

A year later at the Broadway, on the evening of Dec. 6, folks were filing out of the theatre after taking in the Saturday-night vaudeville show with the Broadway Orchestra and a late screening of Clark Gable and Lana Turner's new western, "Honky Tonk."

It would be the last night of normalcy Pitmanites would know for the next four years. The amorous faces of Gable and Turner ("Every Kiss a Thrill!") were still greeting locals out holiday window shopping on Broadway on Sunday afternoon, Dec. 7, 1941, as 353 Japanese aircraft attacked Pearl Harbor, Hawaii, sinking four United States Navy battleships and killing 2,393 Americans. The next afternoon at 12:30 p.m., borough residents gathered around their radios to listen to a six-and-a-half-minute national address to Congress from President Franklin D. Roosevelt.

Within hours, America's entry into World War II would alter life in Pitman forever.

VICTORY
THANKSGIVING
SERVICE

BROADWAY THEATRE

PITMAN · NEW JERSEY

SUNDAY, MAY THIRTEENTH

CHAPTER FOUR

"Let's All Back the Attack!"
1941–1951

Named for the town's only casualty in World War I, Pitman's Elwood Kindle American Legion Post No. 49 and the borough's newly assembled Defense Council had an urgent message for residents. In its Dec. 11, 1941, edition, the Woodbury Daily Times announced an all-hands-on-deck need for able-bodied Pitmanites to operate the new air raid warning station. "Do not delay. Get in line at once." The town's Kiwanis Club, meanwhile, announced it was reallocating the prize money normally awarded for its annual Christmas lights contest to the Pitman ambulance fund. But the club appealed to residents to decorate their homes anyway "as an expression of gratitude for the many blessings we still enjoy in our country."

As an estimated 6,000 Gloucester County residents rushed to enlist (719 of them Pitman residents), Ralph Wilkins, at age 47, a husband, father, theatre owner and borough council member, knew his place was supporting the war effort at home. As the first films of the attack on Pearl Harbor flickered across the Broadway screen in "March of Time" newsreels, MGM's new Jeanette MacDonald and Brian Aherne Technicolor musical "Smilin' Through" attempted to lighten the mood during the 1941 holiday season. Also serving that purpose was the new Humphrey Bogart private eye picture "The Maltese Falcon." Having successfully secured new parking for Pitman, Wilkins retired from politics after a single term. He decided to dedicate all his energies to running the Broadway and leading the town's ambitious war bond fundraising efforts.

A Pitman Grove Review editorial urged readers: "Let's all back the attack! The staggering sum of money necessary for victory of the American and allied forces must be borne in large measure by the American people left at home. Let's not shillyshally or debate. Let's dig deep into our pockets. Let's root those dollars out of the dark today."

Ads in the paper also reminded Pitman residents of their new wartime social obligations. "Minutes matter more in war," cajoled New Jersey Bell Telephone. "When long distance lines are crowded, the operator will say 'please limit your call to five minutes.'" A C.M. Kandle ad advised, "Hoard Heat! Fuel conservation is vital to the war effort. Call us now and let us give you an estimate of insulating walls, your roof and having storm windows and doors added." Pitman National Bank & Trust reminded local farmers that buying war bonds could help finance their postwar crops.

In addition to the town's two banks now serving as war bond centers, as head of the local bond drives, Ralph Wilkins had a booth built at the Broadway so theatregoers could conveniently purchase bonds in the lobby. Wilkins was also taking up regular collections at the theatre to aid the Red Cross War Drive. The Camden Morning Post reported that in September 1942 alone, Ralph Wilkins, Broadway Theatre patrons and Pitman's PTA raised a total of $61,975 in war bonds sold at the theatre.

Between war bond sales and the bloody blitzkrieg attack images unspooling on the "March of Time" newsreels, there were still causes for celebration at the Broadway Theatre. On June 9, proud families filed in to watch 87 members of the Pitman High School senior class of 1942 walk across the stage to receive their diplomas. But other mainstays of the Broadway vanished during the war. Due to rationing, vaudeville was over in America by 1943. As Broadway projectionist Al Beckett later noted, "It was hard to get gasoline and transportation was in sad shape."

On Feb. 2, 1,000 patrons piled into the Broadway Theatre for a private war bond fundraising screening of "Yankee Doodle Dandy," the new George M. Cohan biography starring James Cagney. All attendees were admitted free — if they had purchased a war bond of $50 or more. Onstage, Ralph Wilkins thanked theatre patrons and then introduced Navy man Bill Nichols, a local storekeeper, who'd left his bed at the naval hospital in Philadelphia to tell bond buyers how critical their donations were. Wounded in the South Pacific, Nichols informed the assembled that his former flotilla of naval craft consumed as much fuel in one hour as an ordinary citizen could use for pleasure driving in a lifetime.

Finally, Wadsworth Cresse, who had been hired as cashier at Pitman National Bank when it debuted in 1911 and was now helping to lead the Gloucester County war bond effort, took to the Broadway stage for a final appeal. "Our soldiers don't quit because they've shot several rounds of ammunition," he reminded the crowd. "Six thousand boys from Gloucester County in the armed services are depending on the support war bond buyers can give them. They shouldn't depend alone on God and a fast outfield." By the end of the night, the event had raised $50,000 for the war effort. By the end of the fourth national war bond drive, Pitman alone had raised $308,060.75.

As war raged overseas, Pitman's youngsters continued to grow up. In the summer of 1944, Clayton E. Platt, now 13 and a member of Pitman's Boy Scout Troop 18, was busy earning merit badges in bird study, lifesaving and athletics. As a child watching movies at the Broadway, Pitman native Jane McCausland's first exposure to the horrors of the war was the newsreels. "It was the only way to get news," she remembers. "That's where you saw the planes, the tanks and the trenches. The footage was maybe weeks old by the time you saw it. Throughout the war, the Broadway also served as our entertainment, our relief." During the day, the theatre was also a backyard playground for Warren Carr, who was growing up in the house behind the theatre his grandmother Laura had built in 1927. "As a boy, I was in and out of every inch of that theatre," Carr remembers with a laugh. "Unfortunately, the projection room was always locked, but I got to roam around most of the rest of it."

By November 1944, Ralph Wilkins, who by then was the Gloucester County chairman of the War Activities Committee, Motion Picture Industry, helped lead a meeting of 700 motion picture theatre operators from across the Delaware Valley at the Warwick Hotel in Philadelphia. At the convention, attendees planned 26 consecutive days of war bond drives — the sixth such national initiative — at theatres across the tristate area.

The Woodbury Daily Times praised Wilkins and the volunteer corps of women bond sellers "who have sold hundreds of bonds in the theatre this month and swelled the town's total." At its monthly meeting at Hotel Pitman, the Pitman Kiwanis Club surprised its former president by honoring Wilkins for his dedication to the war effort.

For Christmas 1944, Santa and Ralph Wilkins delivered to Broadway patrons the critically acclaimed war drama "Since You Went Away," starring Claudette Colbert, Jennifer Jones, Joseph Cotten and Shirley Temple, just as Pitman celebrated crossing $336,000 in sales of war bonds (the equivalent of $5.9 million today). Pitmanites were relishing one other holiday gift as well — the tide of the war was continuing to turn in Europe.

In between accepting honors and selling bonds, the owner of the Broadway Theatre also had to oversee life's more mundane tasks. In late January, Wilkins was greeted at the theatre with no heat and 8 feet of water in the basement, courtesy of a frozen and ruptured sprinkler system pipe. After Pitman fire volunteers spent all day Friday pumping water out of the basement, movies — and the heat — resumed on Saturday night.

By February 1945, the Pitman War Memorial Committee was planning a Thanksgiving Service and Victory Celebration to take place at the Broadway Theatre on the Sunday following the official announcement of victory over Germany. On the way to the meeting, committee members walked past a new display in the window of Sy Doughty's

Smoke Shop on Broadway — the cap, jacket, trousers and canteen of a captured Japanese officer. The outfit had been mailed home by local boy Sgt. Hank Horner, on duty in the U.S. Army in the Philippines.

On the front page of the March 15, 1945, edition of the Pitman Grove Review, Ralph Wilkins shared with residents a letter sent to him by a former Broadway vaudeville comic — Bob Hope, who was now a celebrity fundraiser for the American Red Cross. Under the headline "Bob Hope Expresses Appreciation of Efforts by Manager Wilkins," the letter read in part: "Dear Mr. Wilkins, The need of the Red Cross is overwhelming. The purpose of this letter now is only to say to you thanks for agreeing to take up collections at your theatre. Please do so at every performance, for whatever effort you put forth will be much appreciated by those upon whom we have to depend to bring us to a conclusion of this horrible war. Some boy from your town may live because of what you have done. Sincerely, Bob Hope."

The letter from one of America's biggest radio and movie stars resulted in swelled attendance at all the Broadway Red Cross screening fundraisers booked by Wilkins, including the war drama "I'll Be Seeing You," with Ginger Rogers, Joseph Cotten and Shirley Temple; William Powell and Myrna Loy in their final Nick and Nora Charles outing, "The Thin Man Goes Home"; and, perhaps not coincidentally, Bob Hope's new Technicolor comedy with Virginia Mayo, "The Princess and the Pirate." Or as the ad promised, "lovelies and laughs!"

At 9 a.m. on May 8, 1945, Pitmanites once again gathered around the radio. In his address, President Harry S. Truman announced Nazi Germany's unconditional surrender, praising the hard work and sacrifice of the American people but reminding them that the war continued in the Far East. As the Pitman Grove Review noted, Victory in Europe Day was observed quietly in Pitman. A few church bells sounded and the White Star laundry "whistle blew long and loudly." Many stores closed up shop early.

As planned by Pitman's War Memorial Committee, on Sunday afternoon at 2:30, the doors to the Broadway Theatre were opened for a V.E. Day program dedicated to "community rejoicing and prayers of thanksgiving." The Pitman High School Band and Glee Club provided the music, along with soloists Charles Butler, who performed the national anthem and Charles Chauncy, who sang "The White Cliffs of Dover." And Pitmanite C. Austin Miles, best known for composing the popular hymn "In the Garden," led the singing of his latest, "White Crosses," written especially for the occasion.

In late July, some of Pitman's contributions to the victory in Europe were vividly on display in the front window of the town's Webb & Lodge Drug Store. Pitmanite Staff Sergeant Elwood Ewan, as part of the European liberation forces, had personally liberated a few keepsakes. Specifically, a silver cream pitcher with a coat of arms and a large key from Adolf Hitler's palatial home in the Bavarian Alps, following the fuhrer's suicide in Berlin on April 30.

But if V.E. Day proved sedate in Pitman, Victory in Japan Day on Tuesday, Aug. 14, 1945, was anything but. "Far into the night, happy people marched through town, venting their great joy over the war's end," reported the Pitman Grove Review. "Pots, pans, big cans, noisemakers, anything with sound attached was called into service as Broadway rocked with racket. People walked, rode in cars, stood on their porches, waved flags and shouted themselves hoarse." From his parking spot in Ballard Park, Pitmanite Stanton S. Woidill and his sound truck broadcast President Truman's 7 p.m. White House address to residents across town. "God's help has brought us to this day of victory," Truman concluded. "With His help we will attain that peace and prosperity for ourselves and all the world in the years ahead." The town's fire siren and church bells then began ringing. The town's old fire gong rang and the White Star laundry whistle sounded. Over 1,000 flags were distributed by the borough. Streamers and confetti fluttered from cars.

At 9 p.m., Pitman police blocked off Pitman Avenue from Simpson to Broadway. An amplification system was erected on the corner of Ballard Park and dancing commenced on Broadway in front of the theatre and the two banks, where so many war bonds had been sold. "Authorities felt gratified and pleased with the celebrants," the Pitman Grove Review reported, "since so little property damage took place. Police had no accidents on their record on the morning following the big night even if it was probably the most enthusiastic night Pitman has known in its 75 years of existence."

Like the rest of the country, on Wednesday, Aug. 15, Pitman's business district was closed for a two-day national holiday. "In deep contrast to the evening before," observed the Review, "the town was really at peace." On Sunday, Aug. 19, 1945, at 3 p.m., nearly 1,200 attendees packed into the Broadway for the V.J. Day celebration, ushered to their seats by local members of the Boy and Girl Scouts of America. The celebration started with a recital at 2:45 p.m. by Mrs. Isaac Worrall, music director of the Pitman Presbyterian Church, on the theatre's Kimball organ. Palm plants ringed the theatre stage, donated by Merritt's Flowers and arranged personally by Reeves Merritt himself.

Used with permission. Pitman Historical Museum.

"The cessation of hostilities brings all of us at home great joy," Pitman Mayor Melvin C. Webb told attendees in a program note addressed to the more than 700 Pitman service members who had gone to war: "Joy because those of you in the field are relieved of imminent danger. Victory has brought peace to a weary world at a terrible cost paid by you and your comrades. In the name of the community, we salute all of you and welcome your return home as we look forward to your leadership in the days of peace ahead."

On the back of the program, an Honor Roll commemorated the 719 residents who "entered the Nation's Armed Services during World War II" and listed the names of the 19 Pitman residents killed in action during the war and the five who remained missing.

Thanks to Ralph Wilkins' dedicated leadership, the people of Pitman had raised over half a million dollars for the war effort. But for residents, nothing signaled a postwar return to normalcy like the front-page announcement in the Sept. 27, 1945, edition of the Pitman Grove Review. It informed residents that due to the "daily increase of traffic," the borough was reinstituting its one-hour parking regulation in the business district.

The Review observed the Broadway Theatre's 20th anniversary in its May 23, 1946, edition, along with a note from its manager and owner Ralph Wilkins: "In this world of rising prices there is no greater value for one's money than a ticket to one of the shows at the Broadway. We wish to thank the residents of Pitman and vicinity for their splendid support and patronage."

By the time the Broadway Theatre had reached its two-decade milestone, it was no longer just a place to sit in the dark with your sweetheart to watch your favorite Hollywood stars. Through its cooking schools, war bond booths, high school commencements and V.E. Day and V.J. Day celebrations, Pitman's Broadway Theatre was now a community center and an indelible part of the town. It had become not just a place to laugh together at the antics of Donald Duck but also a place to pray for loved ones fighting for freedom in a conflict halfway around the world and to celebrate their safe return.

On May 1-3, 1947, Pitmanites celebrated the return of James Stewart to the silver screen after five years of the actor's flying combat missions as a member of the 2nd Air Division of the Army Air Forces. His first Hollywood assignment after the war — playing George Bailey in director Frank Capra's "It's a Wonderful Life." Accompanying photos of Stewart and Donna Reed in the Broadway newspaper ad was the tagline "Jimmy's New Picture ... And It's Wonderful!"

In a 1987 essay published in Guideposts, Stewart reflected, "As one of the longest American movie sets ever made until then, Bedford Falls had 75 stores and buildings on four acres with a three-block main street lined with 20 full-grown oak trees. It reminded me of my hometown, Indiana, Pennsylvania. But it wasn't the elaborate set that made 'It's a Wonderful Life' so different, it was the story. George Bailey was an ordinary fella who thinks he's never accomplished anything in life. Then an angel takes him back through his life to show how our ordinary everyday efforts are really big achievements."

It would take a full year before Capra's $3.1 million future classic even broke even. He didn't care. "I thought it was the greatest film I had ever made," the director reflected in his autobiography. "I thought it was the greatest film anybody ever made. It was my kind of film for my kind of people. A film that said to the downtrodden, the pushed-around, 'Heads up, fella. No man is poor who has one

1947 Pitman Grove Review ad. Gloucester County Historical Society.

friend. Three friends and you're filthy rich.'"

For many in the audience at the Broadway, the scenes depicting the war effort at home in Bedford Falls mirrored Pitman's response and, in particular, Ralph Wilkins' and the Broadway's home-front contributions throughout the war years.

In the years to come, as motion picture exhibitors faced the scourge of millions of new glowing boxes in living rooms across the country, Ralph Wilkins would rely on that loyalty of local residents as changes in Hollywood roiled the industry.

Hollywood studios, meanwhile, were busy rolling out a series of gimmicks to lure Americans out of their increasingly television-accented living rooms and back into theatres. Warner Bros. was the first Hollywood studio to produce a 3-D thriller, "House of Wax," starring Vincent Price. The movie poster promised: "The Most Astonishing Motion Picture Since Motion Pictures Began! The story of a half-man half-monster who stalked a panic-swept city for the beauties he craved for his chamber of horrors!" Some of the 3-D effects intended to jolt audiences out of their seats included cancan girls, a paddle-ball-wielding carnival barker and one genuine jump scare featuring a shadowy figure appearing to leap from the audience up into the screen.

It's highly likely that "House of Wax," a film that had topped the box office for five straight weeks, was not a personal favorite of Ralph Wilkins'. For starters, he and projectionist Al Beckett had to figure out how to screen the thing. The solution? The purchase of two additional and expensive film projectors. "Most theatres only have two projectors," Beckett later explained to the Gloucester County

1940s Broadway. Used with permission. Gloucester County Historical Society.

Times. "We have four because when three-dimensional pictures came out, we had to run one machine for each eye — two at once. We needed four machines so we wouldn't have to stop the show and reload."

One Hollywood innovation developed to tackle television had a more lasting effect — CinemaScope. But like 3-D, the new widescreen film format required motion picture exhibitors to upgrade their theatres, this time by purchasing new stereophonic sound equipment and installing larger, curved screens. "The Robe," Hollywood's first blockbuster shot in CinemaScope, debuted in New York City on Sept. 16, 1953. By the following January, Wilkins had not only fully upgraded the Broadway but had booked the film adaptation of the Broadway musical "Kiss Me, Kate," which was presented in both 3-D and on the theatre's brand-new

"Wide Screen Curved Panoramic Screen." Or as newspaper ads now reminded readers, "Broadway Theatre, Pitman, Home of CinemaScope Pictures." By spring, Wilkins had upgraded the Glassboro Theatre as well.

1952 invitation to commencement held at the Broadway. From the author's collection.

In junior high, Kevin Austin began working for Wilkins as an usher, a job for which there were two essential requirements — you had to wear a suit and own a flashlight. Austin still remembers hearing the "ding, ding, ding" signal from Beckett in the projection booth when the cartoons and trailers were finished playing on the standard screen. When the main curtain closed, it was time for Austin to sprint into action.

"At the time, there were two screens, because the trailers and cartoons were formatted to fit on the older, smaller screen and the features [shot in CinemaScope] ran on the wider screen," explains Austin. "When you heard that signal, man, you had to race down to the stage and get behind that screen and quickly bring up the smaller one so the feature could begin. You had to be quick, but you couldn't yank on the curtain rope too hard or it went off its track. You'd catch hell for that."

While Wilkins' Glassboro Theatre was screening "The Robe," the Broadway was dazzling audiences with Walt Disney's new CinemaScope-shot "20,000 Leagues Under the Sea," with Kirk Douglas, and the lavish widescreen film adaptation of the Rodgers & Hammerstein musical "The King and I," starring Deborah Kerr and Yul Brynner. (Wilkins billed the run as "Three glorious days, a great show for young and old!")

But another technological marvel was about to impact Pitman even more than CinemaScope – a transformational wonder that would create a fresh and vital role for the town's 25-year-old movie palace.

On Nov. 30, 1951, the 117.2-mile New Jersey Turnpike, the first modern toll road in the state, opened to traffic.

Broadway Theatre owner Ralph Wilkins and wife Elizabeth at Warners' twentieth anniversary of talking pictures celebration in Atlantic City. Photo courtesy of Bonnie Wilkins Dewey.

"Wouldn't You Rather See Movies in Pitman Sunday Evenings?"

1953–1971

The flashbulb-popping midnight scene in front of the Broadway on May 2, 1953, might easily have been mistaken for a Hollywood premiere. Applauding spectators lined the street as young women in gowns and young men in white dinner jackets dashed from vehicles dropping them off at the theatre. Across the street, Pitman Fire Company No. 1's blinding searchlights atop the truck illuminated the action below.

This was the debut of the town's new Prom Night. The occasion was Pitman High School's first-ever after-prom celebration, planned as an all-night affair. The event, 10 months in the making, was the joint brainchild of parents, students and concerned townspeople. Pitman parents were worried the state's new turnpike could lure tired, inexperienced teen drivers into the gravitational pull of New York City. So the town came up with an all-night party chaperoned by parents and designed to keep young people off the roads.

1954 Broadway Theatre program.
From the author's collection.

At the prom's 11 p.m. conclusion outside the Pitman High gymnasium, 50 vehicles awaited the departing couples. In addition to parents, chauffeurs included Pitman's director of public safety, the supervisor of schools, the borough director of finance and even Pitman Mayor Walter S. Gibbs. The promsters were then shuttled to the theatre. But the teens on the planning committee had decided that cheering and taking pictures on the sidewalk would be the extent of the privileges granted to the adults on their special night. Parental figures were not invited inside to see the couples announced as they glided across the Broadway's stage to their classmates' applause. Or to the private screening of the new Humphrey Bogart-June Allyson picture "Battle Circus," set in a Mobile Army Surgical Hospital [M.A.S.H.] unit during the Korean War.

After Jed and Ruth – Bogart and Allyson's characters – were reunited on screen after a perilous escape across enemy lines, cars idling outside the Broadway whisked the high schoolers to the Pitman Masonic hall. Thanks to a lot of work from parents, the venue had been transformed into a teen nightclub, complete with floor show and five-piece band. As a reporter from the Philadelphia Sunday Bulletin observed, "The kids table-hopped, pounded out dance band rhythms with nightclub wooden hammers and perched party hats on each other's heads. And by the time they had worn themselves out, the stars in the heavens had

1967 Pitman High School after-prom celebration. From the author's collection.

gone to sleep." The final stop before bed — a breakfast of scrambled eggs, sausage, coffee and hot chocolate, prepared by parents at the Parish House of the Church of the Good Shepherd.

Other communities were taking note of Pitman's inventive approach to prom night in the modern age of the turnpike. In his front-page May 4, 1953, Vineland Daily Journal column, Ben Leuchter praised the town's creative efforts "to give Pitman teenagers the most exciting – and safest – prom night in history."

By 1956, Pitman's all-night after-prom festivities had gotten so well-known, Bill Haley & His Comets, featured in Columbia Pictures' just-released "Rock Around the Clock," were booked to play the Masonic hall. Pitman teens and their dates not only danced to Haley's global hit but also "Shake, Rattle and Roll" and the band's latest, "See You Later, Alligator."

"Back in those days, you could still get groups like that to play a prom," explains Lee Eldredge, a 1953 Woodbury High graduate, who was going steady with Barbara Schaeffer, a member of Pitman High's class of 1956. "I had bought this real loud sport coat to wear to Barbara's prom. It was multicolored and so bright it was almost iridescent. I thought I was the coolest cat in town. When we got to the gym, we put our coats in the cloakroom. At the end of the prom, I discovered my brand-new jacket was gone and had been replaced by some old raggedy one similar to it! That's the jacket I wore to the Broadway and for the rest of the night. Needless to say, I was a little ticked. But I guess getting to watch Bill Haley and the Comets made up for it."

Thanks to Haley and the birth of rock 'n' roll, youth culture was exploding in the 1950s as Pitman's all-night prom festivities grew in size and scope. On screen at the Broadway, Elizabeth Taylor, Rock Hudson and – in his final picture – James Dean were pulling in the young people with the melodrama "Giant." That film's co-star Sal Mineo was also headlining Universal-International's "Rock, Pretty Baby!" Bill Haley & His Comets were back on the big screen with "Don't Knock the Rock" at the Broadway the same week that James Darren debuted in the juvenile delinquent drama "Rumble on the Docks." Hollywood's current "It" couple, Eddie Fisher and Debbie Reynolds, meanwhile, drew Broadway crowds for their first picture together, "Bundle of Joy." For the more mature Pitmanites like himself, Ralph Wilkins booked the CinemaScope-shot film adaptation of Rodgers & Hammerstein's "Oklahoma!" ("Four Big Days Four!") and Bing Crosby, Grace Kelly and Frank Sinatra in "High Society," the new widescreen musical version of "The Philadelphia Story."

In July 1955, the Broadway was prominently featured as a host venue during Pitman's weeklong Golden Jubilee celebration commemorating the 50th anniversary of the town's 1905 founding. And returning to his hometown for the week's events was none other than Preston Foster, the Hollywood actor and Pitman's biggest hometown celebrity. In 1955, Foster was at the height of his career, portraying Captain John Herrick, a Los Angeles harbor tugboat captain, on the hit weekly TV series "Waterfront." The show was so popular that some viewers were naming their daughters Cheryl Ann, after Captain John's tugboat. On Saturday morning, July 2, a motorcade of cars decorated with red, white and blue bunting left Pitman and drove into the North Philadelphia train station to meet Foster, his wife, Sheila and daughter Stephanie. When Foster and family emerged from the train just after 8 a.m., he was delighted to discover an estimated 600 Pitmanites, including the entire Pitman Hobo Band, waiting for him. On the station platform, Foster happily posed for photos with his sisters and neighbors, who were clutching signs reading "You Can Choose Your Friends But You're Stuck With Us" and "Hi Cap'n John – Love That Man!!"

At the Broadway, the Pitman Lions Club had organized a "Celebrity Night" as its contribution to the town's Golden Jubilee. The shindig was emceed by Philadelphia KYW-AM DJ and Pitman resident Mac McGuire, with Preston Foster the evening's featured performer, along with his wife and daughter. Between "Waterfront" seasons, the Fosters

Actor Preston Foster with 1955 Miss Pitman contestants. From the author's collection.

toured nationally together as a nightclub act. During his visit home, Foster also served as grand marshal of the July 4th parade. Dressed as his TV character Captain John, the actor waved to the crowd aboard a Cheryl Ann tugboat float on a flatbed trailer. Foster also crowned Miss Pitman 1955, Lois Haight, in front of an estimated crowd of 5,000 sitting at Davis Field behind Pitman High School. In an emotional address, Foster told his hometown, "I was never so completely surprised, overwhelmed and honored in all my life as at the reception I received at North Philadelphia station. It has been this way all week. This is the greatest thing that's ever happened to my family or me. I will never forget it."

By 1957, the town's annual after-prom event had become such a fixture on the town's calendar, Pitman Grove Review writer Bud Emery was routinely covering it. And in a victory for the Pitman parents forgoing sleep to chauffeur their offspring around town all night, the After-Prom Committee had decided parents and other guests could purchase a ticket to observe the festivities at the theatre — from the Broadway's balcony. At the Masonic hall, Philadelphia radio station WIP was broadcasting live as sophomore Beverly Barrett, dressed as a nightclub cigarette girl, sold candy cigarettes to her older classmates, who paid her in chocolate tin-foiled coins. Onstage, the Four Aces performed their hits "Three Coins in the Fountain," "Mr. Sandman" and "Love Is a Many Splendored Thing." The singing group then ceded the stage to the morning's headliners, the Everly Brothers, who were burning up the charts with "Bye Bye Love" and "Wake Up Little Susie."

Gayle Butler, who attended the prom in 1957 and 1958, recalls, "I know it was a tremendous amount of work, but it certainly kept the kids safe. We were finally driven home about 6 or 7 o'clock in the morning, totally exhausted but with wonderful memories that lasted a lifetime." Adds Les Butler: "I will never forget, the Everly Brothers were on 'Ed Sullivan' a couple weeks after our prom. We also got coverage in Life magazine. It was so special!" Another Pitman High promgoer, Mary Anne Pryzma, reflects, "I have never heard of anybody's prom that topped ours! Nowadays, the kids pay a lot for the clothes, the limo, the dinner and no after-prom or photos. And wasn't it something to have so much parental support — staying up all night to chauffeur us."

The town's all-night after-prom tradition, complete with private early-morning screenings at the Broadway, continued for the next 20 years, well into the 1970s.

By May 20, 1957, the Broadway's 31st anniversary, the young recording artists that Ralph Wilkins was bringing to the theatre's stage were a far cry from the jugglers and acrobats of vaudeville days. He was also booking double features of Hollywood's popular sci-fi B-pictures, including "Attack of the Crab Monsters" on a bill with "Not of This Earth" and "The Giant Claw," paired with "The Night the World Exploded!"

"Ralph was a good businessman," says Warren Carr. "He also cared about his community. If the theatre was open, he was there. His green four-door Studebaker would be parked outside. He was a quiet guy and not someone looking to get his name in the papers. He just went to work. He wanted the Broadway to make money."

Adds Bobbi Snelbaker Wilkins, who grew up a few blocks from the Broadway and married Ralph Wilkins' grandson Robert in 1961: "Pop-Pop, as I called him, was only maybe 5-foot-6 and always had on a gray suit and a tie. He was pretty straitlaced. I don't think I ever heard him use a curse word. He loved his big cabin cruiser boat on Wildwood Crest. He named it DEBRA — the D was for Doris, his daughter-in-law, E for [his wife] Elizabeth, B for [his son] Bob and RA for Ralph. On Wednesdays, he took off from the theatre and many of the businesses closed at noon — the jeweler, the butcher, the pharmacist all went fishing with him on Pop-Pop's boat."

While Pitman's under-10 set was excited to visit with Santa in Ballard Park during the 1957 holiday season, at the Broadway Ralph Wilkins had booked a very special pelvic-thrusting present for the bigger kids — Elvis Presley's new hit film "Jailhouse Rock," "featuring 7 sizzling new songs from MGM in CinemaScope." Debra Moore Higbee, a Pitman native who would grow up to serve on the borough council and work as a longtime librarian at Walls Elementary, recalls going on her first movie date to see "Flipper" at the Broadway and receiving a free 45 rpm record of heartthrob Gene Pitney's "(The Man Who Shot) Liberty Valance" when she went to see the 1962 James Stewart-John Wayne western at the theatre. "I still have that 45," she says. "For years, we had a jukebox and it was one of the records we had in it."

By 1960, Ralph Wilkins, at 66, had watched his son Robert and daughter-in-law Doris successfully transplant their small Pitman wholesale flower business into the budding Delaware Valley Wholesale Florists in Sewell. The DVWF would eventually bloom into a nationally recognized wholesale flower industry leader. Other kids Wilkins had served popcorn to at the Broadway throughout the decades were also growing up and becoming local leaders. In neighboring Glassboro, Clayton E. Platt, who had first started coming to the Broadway as a boy in the 1930s, was being sworn in as a Glassboro councilman. A lifelong movie fan, the man nicknamed "Duffy" by friends was intent on acquiring Wilkins' High Street movie house. By 1962, Platt had not only become the proprietor of the Glassboro Theatre, but when Alfred Hitchcock's thriller "The Birds" played the Levoy Theatre in Millville in 1963, his newly formed Platt Theatres Inc. owned that venue as well.

Hotel Pitman postcard. From the author's collection.

As he navigated fresh competition from the next generation of theatre owners, Wilkins took the night off in March 1966 to attend the Pitman Business Men's Association's gathering at Hotel Pitman, where he was awarded its Man of the Year Award "for his 40 years of outstanding service to the community." Toastmaster and insurance agency owner Len Eckman described Wilkins and the Broadway Theatre as "doing more to bring people to Pitman than any other. Ralph asked nothing and gave much and deserves great credit for his continued selection of the best in films."

The same could not be said for Wilkins' new competitor over on High Street in Glassboro. Early in his run as the owner of the Glassboro Theatre, Platt had hosted a live appearance with Happy the Clown for the town's kiddie population. But by the summer of 1968, the fare he was booking at Ralph Wilkins' former theatre was decidedly more adult.

Platt had begun screening X-rated films with titles like "Deep Inside" and "No One Under 18 Admitted" signs posted out front, along with edgy Hollywood fare like "The Graduate" and "Valley of the Dolls." In Pitman, Ralph Wilkins booked "Stay Away, Joe," one of Elvis Presley's final films, as the singer's long studio contract with MGM limped to an end.

Some of Ken Wilkins' earliest memories revolve around Saturdays spent with his sister Bonnie and their great-grandfather Ralph at the Broadway. "The organ would be going, the seats were plush and comfortable and you felt like you were in a truly special place," recalls Wilkins, who was born in 1964. "My great-grandfather would let us into the theatre early and I would watch him put these giant blocks of butter into this heated pot to melt for the popcorn."

Broadway organist Robert M. Figlio.
Photo courtesy of Nathan Figlio.

Nathan Figlio, the son of Robert M. Figlio, the Broadway's organist in the 1960s, also had full run of the theatre as a kid. "Mr. Wilkins kind of reminded me of a school principal," Nathan remembers. "But he was always very kind to my sister and me. He would buy us Necco wafers out of the candy machine. It was his little gift to us whenever we visited. We thought that was wonderful."

With a pipe organ to practice on at home, Nathan was warming to the family business. He especially remembers a rerelease engagement of "The Sound of Music" at the Broadway where his father, along with pipe organ icons Lowell Ayars and Esther Higgins, performed a week of one-hour concerts prior to the movie. By 1968, as other old movie houses died off, the Broadway's Kimball theatre organ was the last of its kind in operation in South Jersey.

"I think it was sometimes tough for Mr. Wilkins to make ends meet at that point," recalls Kevin Austin, who worked at the Broadway all through high school in the late 1960s. "Things were changing, business had declined. Mr. Wilkins was frugal and a hard worker. As an usher, you had to throw people out if they didn't behave. I mostly worked the balcony on Friday and Saturday. Inevitably, the emergency door would get kicked open and kids would rush inside, sometimes my friends. And the second that outside light came pouring into the theatre? Mr. Wilkins would be right there asking, 'Who's that?' It was my job to try and catch them!"

On Tuesday nights, rechargeable flashlight in hand, Austin worked the early show as an usher and then it was his job to change the marquee out front with the title of the new week's feature. Writing down both the current and next feature, Austin then dashed downstairs to select the red letters he'd need before heading out to the Broadway sidewalk with a 10-foot ladder. Al Beckett had also taught the high schooler how to run the projectors.

In order to stay competitive and coax younger Pitman-ites back in the door (paying ones, that is), Wilkins booked the demonic-possession psychological horror hit "Rosemary's Baby," starring Mia Farrow and, later, Warren Beatty and Faye Dunaway's bullets-and-blood-soaked "Bonnie and Clyde," both rated R. Bobbi Wilkins, Ralph's granddaughter-in-law, was among the young people who went to see "Bonnie and Clyde" at the Broadway. "As movies got more risqué in the '60s, he wasn't always happy about it," she recalls. "But that's what sold, so Pop-Pop booked them. No matter what was on the screen, there he would be, standing in the back of the theatre. I don't know if he ever sat down."

But Wilkins' ongoing challenge of trying to secure crowd-pleasing, family-friendly films in the age of Hollywood's counterculture for a town founded by Methodists fell by the wayside on the afternoon of Aug. 17, 1968.

At half past noon, Highland Chemical Fire Co. volunteer firefighter George W. Kelly Jr. was at his mother's house on Delsea Drive building cabinets. That's when he saw his fellow firefighters race past. They had been radioed about a fire, so Kelly got in his pickup and followed them.

Inside Cobbin Jewelers, the shop next door to the Broadway Theatre, Everett Silverman was waiting on a customer at the counter when he smelled smoke. Hurrying patrons out of the store, Silverman discovered the basement ablaze. By the time Pitman volunteer firefighters arrived minutes later, the flames were threatening the adjacent businesses, Pitman Hardware, Huberty's Pharmacy and the apartments above. A ladder truck was quickly set up in the middle of Broadway and firefighters began pumping water on the upper stories.

Wearing masks and air packs, George Kelly, along with Harold Mitton, Pete Kandle, Gene Mathis and his brother Harold (the sons of Monte Mathis, the former Hunt's Park Theatre projectionist) entered the burning store. As they groped their way through the smoke toward the rear of the store, the floor suddenly gave way. Kandle frantically tried to grab Kelly as the floor disintegrated, sending Kelly through the flames and into the basement as a heavy display case crashed through the floor on top of him. Kandle was tossed into a door jamb as Gene Mathis was blown over a counter. "There was a heat explosion that bowled us over and almost blew us out of the place," Kandle later recounted to the Woodbury Daily Times.

Chief of patrol Coxie Brown and other firefighters dashed into the building with hose protection, but the exploding flames quickly forced them back onto Broadway. Packing up his family for a trip to the shore, Pitman resident Dr. Edward Wozniak heard the sirens and quickly got downtown. He was immediately positioned at an ambulance to treat injuries and smoke inhalation as firefighters staggered out of the burning building. Downtown business owners hurried pitchers of water, iced tea and wet towels over to the scene. The Sun Ray drugstore sent down salt tablets to be dispensed to the firefighters.

At the height of the three-hour, four-alarm fire in the center of Pitman's business district, an estimated 250 firefighters were on Broadway battling the flames. When the fire was finally extinguished, Kelly, 32, of Kenton Avenue, a married father of three, was dead and eight firefighters were injured. Two storefronts were badly burned. While heavily damaged by water, Huberty's Pharmacy somehow remained intact.

Miraculously, the fire wall separating the Broadway Theatre, erected 42 years earlier, held. The theatre's Saturday-evening show was canceled due to smoke seeping into the theatre.

August 22, 1968, edition of the Pitman Grove Review. Gloucester County Historical Society.

The entire town came together to honor George Kelly Jr.'s life and his ultimate sacrifice at a high Mass held August 21 at Pitman's Our Lady of Peace Roman Catholic Church. A plaque was later erected at 41 S. Broadway memorializing the firefighter. It reads: "On This Site Firefighter George W. Kelly, Jr. of the Highland Chemical Engine Company Gave His Life In The Line Of Duty During The Cobbin Jewelry Store Fire, August 17, 1968." By Thanksgiving, Cobbin Jewelers had rebuilt and reopened to customers. But a year later, the struggling shop closed for good.

Next door, at the theatre, Ralph Wilkins was facing a fresh problem. Pitman's borough council had ordered the theatre's fourth annual Larry Ferrari benefit organ concert canceled. Ferrari was a beloved organist who hosted a weekly organ music program on WPVI-TV. Since 1966, Ferrari had been the star attraction at the theatre's famed Kimball organ for the annual Sunday event benefiting the nearby Elmer Community Hospital. But in March 1969, the borough, citing its 1927 Sunday blue law prohibiting "professional games, sports, plays, performances or shows" on the Sabbath, abruptly canceled the benefit.

Larry Ferrari, WPVI-TV organist. From the author's collection.

Having already sold 400 tickets, the 12-woman Pitman Auxiliary promptly petitioned the borough for a variance. And in response, at its monthly meeting, the council promptly upheld its ordinance. "We have $300 in the treasury and our concert expenses are more than that," pleaded Edna Rash, spokeswoman for the auxiliary. "We did not deliberately go against the ordinance." Pitman Mayor Robert M. Shoemaker told Rash, "We're completely in sympathy with your problem. But the ordinance is explicit and concise." Added Warren Carr, borough solicitor, in the Woodbury Daily Times: "You are holding a professional performance. Admission will be charged. I see no practical way to get around the ordinance."

Ralph Wilkins, who had run the town's premier public gathering place for 43 years, served Pitman as borough councilman and business leader and helped raise over half a million dollars in bonds during the war, had reached his breaking point with the archaic law. Just two years earlier at the Man of the Year ceremony, insurance agency owner Len Eckman had praised him as a man who "asked nothing and gave much."

At age 75, Wilkins decided it was finally time to ask for something.

His flagging theatre needed the financial revenue Sunday hours could offer. At Pitman's VFW and American Legion halls, the theatre owner immediately found allies in his mission to amend the Sunday blue law via a fall ballot referendum. Both organizations had seen a drop in attendance at their monthly Saturday-night dances after Pitman cops had begun showing up to enforce the ordinance at 11:59 p.m. The Sunday blue law had not been enforced in years, but after the VFW and American Legion halls quietly began extending their Saturday-night dances from 1 a.m. to 2 a.m., the borough cracked down. That's when the benefit at the Broadway got caught in the middle. After the canceled Larry Ferrari concert made headlines, it reignited public interest in the Sunday ordinance. Reasoned American Legion Elwood Kindle Post 49 member George Diem, "If they retain [the blue law] as is, every organist in church could be stopped because they are professional performers." Adds Bobbi Wilkins, the theatre owner's granddaughter-in-law: "It's not surprising Pop-Pop was able to mobilize the businessmen. He knew everyone in town."

Publicly, as the town's solicitor, Warren Carr had to legally uphold the ordinance on the books. But privately, Carr, a fellow boating enthusiast, had become friends with Wilkins and supported the theatre owner's efforts. "I used to tell the council, 'In today's world, we have to become economically savvy,'" recalls Carr. "'We have to allow these investments to work for us seven days a week, not just five or six.'"

In the fall of 1969, Pitman had 5,164 registered voters and Wilkins appealed to them directly in a Pitman Grove Review ad, urging them to repeal the town's antiquated law. "To The Voters Of Pitman: Wouldn't you rather see movies in Pitman Sunday evenings than travel out of town? Except for Ocean City, the Broadway Theatre here in Pitman is the only theatre in South Jersey remaining closed on Sundays because of Blue Laws."

In the ad's final paragraph, Wilkins bared his knuckles a bit: "It is harmful to the health of this theatre that it be kept closed. To perpetuate the continued operation of the Broadway Theatre ... VOTE YES to the No. 2 Question: 'Should the Laws of Pitman be amended to permit public assemblies, sporting events and movies on Sundays after the hour of 12 noon?'" Assessing his great-grandfather's messaging 56 years later, Ken Wilkins says, "In that ad, he was strongly suggesting if you don't vote 'Yes,' this movie theatre might close and you won't be able to go to the movies on *any* day in Pitman."

The following Tuesday, Pitmanites demonstrated decisiveness on the issue. The referendum won handily, with 2,131 voters supporting the measure while 1,441 opposed, successfully overturning the old Sunday blue law. But since the referendum was nonbinding, it remained up to the Pitman borough council to strike down the 42-year-old law. Not surprisingly, the Dec. 8 council meeting was packed for the 30-minute public hearing on the issue. Councilman Theodore Jones opposed overturning the ordinance, concurring with a letter he read from concerned citizens Mr. and Mrs. Edwin Erickson: "Pitman has always been just a bit nicer than many other towns. If it becomes the same as other towns on Sunday, it may become like other towns the other six days of the week." Pitman resident Benjamin Hitchner showed up in person to voice his displeasure. "Tradition everywhere is under attack," Hitchner told the assembled. "The question here is the quality of life in Pitman."

1970 Broadway Theatre program.
From the collection of Ralph J. Richards Jr.

Minutes later, when the referendum came to a vote, concerned residents like Hitchner and Councilman Jones were outgunned 4-to-1 by the council in favor of overturning the Sunday blue law. Mayor Robert Shoemaker announced the about-face was "the will of the people." In his first January 1970 ad for the Broadway Theatre, Ralph Wilkins took a well-earned victory lap, announcing at the top: "Now Open Sunday Eves." At the bottom, Wilkins signed this note: "The management of The Broadway Theatre thanks the voters of Pitman who acted favorably for Sunday movies and an appreciation to the Mayor and Council of Pitman who endorsed their vote." And on Sunday, April 19, 1970, Larry Ferrari was once again seated behind the Kimball organ at the Broadway for his annual benefit concert. "Publicly, I didn't take a position either way, but I was not at all surprised the referendum passed," reflects Warren Carr. "Ralph Wilkins was a very honorable guy."

"My great-grandfather's legacy is, he did what he had to do to reinvent the business, reinvest in the business and, yes, occasionally fight with the town for Sunday hours," says Ken Wilkins. "It all reflects not only his love of that theatre but his love for the town of Pitman."

The Broadway's current organist, Nathan Figlio, remains amused by the incident. "It's kind of mind-blowing to realize Larry Ferrari, the guy your grandmother watched on TV and the Broadway's Kimball organ had a role in repealing Pitman's Sunday blue law! There's still a newspaper clipping about it posted in the Broadway's projection booth."

Over on High Street in Glassboro, Clayton E. Platt was also in the news. On its March 12, 1970, front page, the Woodbury Daily Times reported that the owner of the Glassboro Theatre had been shot twice at point blank range while working in the box office by an assailant who fled on foot. Two Glassboro State students, hearing gunshots, helped Platt inside and called an ambulance. With bullet wounds to his leg, forearm and abdomen, Platt was taken to Underwood Memorial and listed in guarded condition after undergoing surgery. A 22-year-old suspect and his 21-year-old brother were later arrested after the duo robbed a Girard Bank in Philadelphia. The triggerman was charged with Platt's attempted murder.

By May 26, Platt was well enough to respond to a Paulsboro resident who had written a letter to the editor of the

Times, upset after her local theatre had screened the X-rated "Midnight Cowboy." The reader cautioned that Paulsboro could turn into "another Glassboro Theatre." By now, Platt's decision to regularly run X-rated films had incurred the ire of residents. In his published response, Platt cited that out of the 91 films he had screened at the Glassboro since the voluntary Motion Picture Association of America ratings system had begun in 1968, only 20 were X-rated. Platt then added, "Our audiences are composed of people from all walks of life, who come of their own free will. If some people had their way, they'd legislate out of business even stores that sell bikini bathing suits, as caterers to pornography."

Platt's pugilistic nature and his defense of screening X-rated films on First Amendment grounds would earn him supporters (many of whom were young people attending nearby Glassboro State College), along with detractors from the local church community. If Clayton "Duffy" Platt represented the future of movie theatre ownership in the 1970s, William C. Hunt, the man who had brought the movies to Pitman in 1913 via his Hunt's Park Theatre on West Jersey Avenue, surely represented a bygone era. On July 12, 1970, Hunt died at age 98. Remembered the Courier-Post, "Owning a string of theatres throughout the state, Mr. Hunt was a pioneer in motion picture enterprises."

Two days later, Pitman's most famous Hollywood export, Preston Foster, died in La Jolla, California, at age 69. In all, Foster had made more than 120 Hollywood pictures, 78 episodes of the TV show "Waterfront" and 100 films for television. Local services were held for the actor at the United Presbyterian Church. Foster and his weeklong participation in Pitman's 1955 Golden Jubilee celebration would be fondly remembered in the 1980 book "Pitman: A Town For All Seasons," commemorating the borough's 75th anniversary Diamond Jubilee.

Just seven months later, on Feb. 24, 1971, Ralph Wilkins, the man who had opened, owned and operated Pitman's Broadway Theatre for 45 years, was also gone, following complications from gallbladder surgery. Wilkins, who had brought silent pictures to Green's Opera House and, later, the Rialto Theatre in Woodbury with his father, Howard, beginning in 1918, was dead at age 77. In addition to his wife, Elizabeth Steward Wilkins and his son, Robert, Wilkins left behind two grandchildren, two great-grand-children and three generations of grateful movie fans. Following a service at Kelley Funeral Home in Pitman, the beloved Broadway Theatre owner and operator was laid to rest at Hillcrest Memorial Park. The Woodbury Daily Times' service club editor H. George Kerby wrote of Wilkins, "Ralph was respected for his business acumen and high ethical standards. His solicitude for the children of the community was shown in the high type of programs in his theatre. His generosity was demonstrated in his free Christmas week children's programs and in his offering the use of his theatre, free of charge, for many community activities."

Added Pitman Kiwanis Club secretary Henry B. Cooper of their former president, "Ralph Wilkins' life stands as a splendid example to our youth and to all the businessmen who knew him." In his "Cy Cez" column, Cy Eastlack wrote, "The 45 years he owned and operated Pitman's Broadway Theatre probably made Ralph Wilkins one of the best-known men throughout South Jersey. Ralph's death hones away another of the remaining few Pitman business pioneers."

Over on Pitman's East Holly Avenue, inside the house they shared for 45 years, a grieving Elizabeth Wilkins had some difficult decisions to make about her late husband's aging movie house. Since 1926, along with the help of staff, Ralph Wilkins had been responsible for everything, from knowing the peculiarities of the air-conditioning system to discerning which of the increasingly provocative films emerging from Hollywood would be suitable for screening in Pitman. On April 29, 1971, with counsel from son Robert and his wife, Doris, now the owners of the successful Delaware Valley Floral Group, Betty Wilkins arrived at a decision.

Ralph Wilkins' widow sold the Broadway Theatre for $110,000. The buyer? A 40-year-old Glassboro resident who at age 8 had first laughed at the antics of Edgar Bergen and Charlie McCarthy at the Broadway with his grandmother in 1939.

The Broadway Theatre's new owner was Clayton E. Platt.

1970 movie poster. From the author's collection.

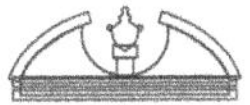

CHAPTER SIX

"I really didn't think I was showing an X-rated movie, to tell you the truth."
1971–1978

Driving through snow flurries on his way to the Broadway, two things likely crossed Pitman Mayor Robert Shoemaker's mind: (1.) This was not how he wanted to spend Valentine's night 1973; and (2.) Clayton Platt was no Ralph Wilkins. Stepping out of his car, Shoemaker looked up at the Broadway's familiar red marquee letters, which spelled out "Double Feature," followed by the letter "X." Inside the theatre, the 7 p.m. feature was underway.

On screen, a café patron rounds a corner carrying a tray of drinks and collides with a nude woman, sending the contents of his tray flying in slow motion. After doing a double-take, the shocked man slowly turns his head and leers at the camera as the title of the United Artists release appears: "What Do You Say to a Naked Lady?" Moments later, businessmen waiting for an elevator are similarly surprised when the doors open and a naked woman emerges to ask for directions.

The X-rated film was "Candid Camera" creator Allen Funt's hidden-lens directorial debut. Freed from the confines of television's rigid standards and practices, Funt's film sought to examine attitudes and reactions to sex, nudity and morality "Candid Camera"-style, largely for cringe-inducing laughs. The comic documentary had been released to theatres hoping to ride the successful sexual revolution wave of the early 1970s, when books like "The Joy of Sex" were becoming bestsellers.

In 1970 and 1971, the titillating film played to packed movie houses around South Jersey. The venues had advertised the film with its X rating and the phrase "Adults Only," letting patrons know this was a racy theatrical release from TV's "Candid Camera" guy. In contrast, in his 1973 newspaper ads, Clayton Platt promoted only the picture's title without its rating. The United Artists movie posters displayed under the Broadway marquee included the X rating, along with the tagline "In This Age of Enlightenment, You Never Know What's Coming Off Next."

In Pitman, what came off next was "What Do You Say to a Naked Lady?" from the town's movie screen after an abbreviated two-day run. Shoemaker had successfully reached "a gentleman's agreement" with the new owner of the Broadway to cancel the rest of the film's run in Pitman. For its front-page story, Shoemaker told the Woodbury Daily Times that Platt had described his film selection to him "as a case of economics." Added Pitman United Methodist Church's Rev. George Propert: "My response is certainly one of displeasure." Of the flap, Platt later reflected to The Philadelphia Inquirer in 1985, "I really didn't think I was showing an X-rated movie, to tell you the truth. Today, it would be rated R."

Sitting in his Cooper Street office in Woodbury, Warren Carr, Pitman's solicitor in 1973, supplies an addendum to the story. "I can distill for you what the 'gentleman's agreement' was. I threatened Platt with an injunction if he didn't stop playing an X-rated film in Pitman. The threat was sufficient. He was not the type of guy you'd invite to a tea party. He didn't believe in discussions, negotiations or understandings. You had to go in and hit him in the head with a mallet. Duffy was not a personality you could easily deal with."

Duffy Platt's film bookings were also causing problems in Glassboro. In December 1973, as both the owner of the Glassboro Theatre and the town's highway administrator, Platt got hauled in front of the mayor and borough council after his successful two-week run of "Deep Throat," the first-ever $1 million-grossing porn film. To the dismay of some residents, Platt had screened the much-talked-about 61-minute film nightly at 7, 8:15, 9:30 and 10:45 p.m., running ads in the Daily Times with the tagline "If you like head, you'll love throat."

Glassboro Mayor William L. Dalton told Platt he had to choose between being the owner of a movie house showing X-rated films or his $7,500-a-year job with the borough. Platt explained he had invested too much in his theatre properties to give them up. Councilman Donald Barger then informed Platt he didn't intend to have Glassboro christened "the pornography capital of the county." In response, Platt pulled out his recent box office receipts, explaining he had grossed $495 from screening Disney's "Bedknobs and Broomsticks" starring Angela Lansbury, while "Deep Throat," with Linda Lovelace, brought in $3,000. Barger then pointedly asked Platt to consider striking with Glassboro the same gentleman's agreement he had made earlier in the year with Pitman Mayor Robert Shoemaker. Platt told him he had agreed to the deal with Shoemaker before New Jersey's new state law on pornography had been ruled unconstitutional in July 1973. "I live by the law," Platt told Barger.

The law notwithstanding, on Dec. 29, picketers, many carrying Bibles and signs proclaiming "Platt Supports Indecency," had gathered beneath the Glassboro Theatre marquee just before the 7 p.m. screening. The dozen or so members of MOTOREDE (Movement To Restore Decency) had been organized by Glassboro resident Bob Dufala, who ran a children's nursery across the street. The latest film being objected to was the Marlon Brando drama "Last Tango in Paris," which carried an X rating for its explicit sex scenes.

As cars drove past with college students yelling at the protesters, Dufala told a reporter that parents dropping off their children at his daycare frequently complained about the movies being shown across the street. Dufala was also accusing Platt of using his borough-owned highway administrator truck to pick up X-rated films for his theatre business. The owner himself was not present. He was busy at the Broadway in Pitman, which was currently playing "Jesus Christ Superstar." After the protests appeared on the front pages of South Jersey newspapers, business was so brisk Platt held over "Last Tango" in Glassboro.

As Platt fought at the next Glassboro council meeting to keep his day job, MOTOREDE protesters followed him through the door of borough hall. Others in attendance argued that Platt's borough job shouldn't be at stake because of objections to the operations of his theatre. Former borough solicitor Harris Y. Cotton had warned the council that establishing Glassboro as a plaintiff in a potential landmark pornography ruling — a case that could go all the way to the Supreme Court — would be costly. On Feb. 12, after the Glassboro Chamber of Commerce wrote a letter on his behalf, the council voted to retain Platt as highway administrator.

When Platt became the second owner of the 45-year-old Broadway in 1971, he had initially tried to ingratiate himself with Pitmanites, announcing his intention to bring live stage shows back to the theatre, a venue he touted as "acoustically perfect." Asked later about his motivations for buying the Broadway, Platt's answer was twofold — he fondly recalled coming to the theatre Saturday nights with his grandmother Mary to see the vaudeville acts in the 1930s; and, he conceded, "I guess I bought it to keep away the competitors."

Platt also acknowledged that movie theatre ownership had changed drastically since his childhood. "It's a cutthroat business," he explained. "Film companies discriminate against the smaller theatres. Whoever pays the most gets the picture. A lot of times, you may not want to show a film, but it's all you have." He explained that many families no longer went to the movies together and consequently, musicals and other family films no longer attracted big crowds. "Violence runs rampant in all of the new pictures. Maybe it's one way for people to work out their frustrations because these films tell it like it is."

Beginning in 1972, the Broadway's competition doubled, thanks to the arrival of the College I and College II twin theatres in the popular Collegetown shopping center.

The twin screens were strategically placed between Platt's movie houses in Pitman and Glassboro. With a nation now enduring odd/even days for purchasing gas due to shortages and record-high inflation, Platt highlighted $1 bargain nights at the Broadway. He theorized to a reporter, "People can't afford to go out to dinner, but they can pay $1."

Occasionally, a film would capture the zeitgeist of the times and keep audiences coming nightly for weeks. In 1974, Platt held over director George Lucas' 1962-set "American Graffiti" for five weeks, running it more than 100 times. The coming-of-age film attracted a wide demographic of both nostalgic adults and teens drawn to the film's young actors, including Ron Howard and Harrison Ford. Platt cited the film as the most popular he had booked during his ownership — until Lucas followed up his box office hit four years later with a sci-fi film titled "Star Wars."

While trying to find the next "American Graffiti" in the ever-eclectic era of 1970s cinema, Platt also needed to hire new projectionists after Al Beckett, the Broadway's longest-serving staffer and projectionist of nearly 50 years, endured a series of health setbacks. "I've had a stroke, a heart attack and I'm diabetic," Beckett, clad in his trademark gray sweatshirt and Dickies khaki work pants, recounted to a Daily Times reporter. "Or is it diabolic? I forget which. But I'm too stubborn to retire. We're only here for a short time between birth and death and I find people who are afraid to live are also afraid to die. People should wake up and start living. Find something to do that you like."

Picking up the slack for Beckett in the projection booth were Platt employees like Kevin Austin, who had started working for Ralph Wilkins pushing a broom at the Broadway in junior high. Now in college, Austin routinely ran the projection in Pitman and Glassboro. "It was a good job for a college student," Austin reflects. "I'd work for five minutes and then I could sit down next to the projector and study for 13 minutes until you had to start the next reel."

Austin was also getting an education in 1970s filmmaking. "This was when all of the Mel Brooks movies were coming out. On the first night I would play them, I remember thinking they were the stupidest things I had ever seen. But having to sit through them so many times, I figured out why they were so funny. His films were made for repeat watching." At age 12, Nathan Figlio, the son of the Broadway's organist, also instantly became a Brooks fan when he got to see "Blazing Saddles" at the theatre. "I remember my stepmother asking Duffy Platt, 'Is this movie OK for kids?' and Duffy telling her, 'Aw, gee, I don't know. There's this one scene where they're eating beans. ...' Out of everything in that movie, Duffy was concerned about the bean scene!"

Having worked for both Wilkins and Platt, projectionist Austin recognized the distinct personality differences between the two Broadway owners. One night when the Broadway ran out of popcorn, Platt called in a favor with the owner of the Grand Theatre Williamstown. Platt handed Austin the keys to his big blue Cadillac sitting out front and told him to go pick up the needed supplies. Recalls Austin, "When I got to Williamstown, this guy hands me a big bag of popcorn and says, 'Tell Duffy Platt to kiss my ass.' When I got back, I made the mistake of passing that message along to Mr. Platt." In response, Platt promptly drove them both back to the Grand. Marching inside, Platt hurled the large sack of popcorn at the owner and stormed out. Reflects Austin decades later: "I remember thinking to myself, 'Kevin, you really need to keep your mouth shut.'"

Finally, by the end of 1976, citing his declining health, Broadway projectionist Al Beckett retired from the booth he had worked in since 1928, steadfastly scrawling the theatre's history on the right-hand wall. In his final inscription, Beckett remembered the first film he'd ever screened at the Broadway in 1928, a silent epic about a boxer whose budding romance is jeopardized by the start of World War I. Wrote Beckett: "'Patent Leather Kid,' 1928. That's 48 years ago tonight, Buster."

Longtime Broadway projectionist Al Beckett. Photo by Mervin D. Chew. Courtesy of the Broadway Theatre.

While screening X-rated films down the street from a college was keeping the lights on at the Glassboro Theatre, Platt had learned the hard way that such content would not fly in a borough founded as a summer church camp. But he had to do something — and fast. In 1975, the future of the Broadway Theatre and the entire Pitman business district was being threatened by the Deptford Mall. The just-opened, million-square-feet indoor shopping emporium 10 minutes up Route 42 contained 125 stores and multiple restaurants.

Michael D. Batten Jr. had been cutting hair at Joe's Barber Shop on Broadway since 1968 and immediately took stock of the changes downtown. "It used to be that people got paid on Friday and then they went downtown to eat at the restaurants and shop," says Batten. "But after the mall opened, little by little, each of those businesses died. The staples like Bob's Hobbies, Pownall's News Agency and the barber shops continued. But when I first moved to Pitman, we had a Woolworth's and clothing stores. Each of those went away and you could see downtown suffering." Adds Pitman native Mike Doughty, who was growing up in town as the mall began to erode Pitman's Uptown, "If you look at the history of the business district, we had an Acme grocery, a Grant's [department store] and shoe shops. It was a self-sufficient little town. If you needed a tailored suit, you might need to drive out of town. Otherwise, you could pretty much buy everything you needed right there on Broadway. Now the town had to find its way as it shifted away from a service economy."

By the end of 1976, the mall was showing first-run films on four screens at the brand-new Deptford Mall Cinema as well. Meanwhile, Duffy Platt's biggest day of the week was the Saturday-afternoon children's matinees, where admission was 50 cents a head and he had to ride herd on a theatre full of mostly unchaperoned, sugar-rush-afflicted small fry all afternoon. Things were so tight, he had taken to standing by the front door to question the kids sneaking candy in from Pownall's across the street instead of buying it at his concession stand.

But just beyond the theatre's silver screen, Platt had something the Deptford Mall couldn't match, even with its fancy new chlorinated fountain — the Broadway's original

1926 vaudeville stage, erected in an acoustically engineered theatre with perfect sight lines. By Thanksgiving weekend 1977, a local promoter had persuaded Platt to book country star Donna Fargo, who had achieved a crossover country hit in 1972 with "The Happiest Girl in the Whole U.S.A." Platt rolled the dice and wrote a check. But by Thanksgiving Eve, he was convinced he had made a serious mistake.

"We were sitting in a tour bus on a highway median, stuck in an ice and snow storm somewhere in Colorado!" remembers Fargo. "I remember thinking, 'Oh Lord, how are we gonna get out of this?'" Forty eight hours before her Pitman debut, Fargo's husband, Stan Silver, was on the phone breaking the bad news to Platt. On Thanksgiving Day, Platt managed to locate and rent replacement equipment for the concert. On Friday, he personally picked up Fargo and her entourage at the Philadelphia airport. But her band's tour bus was still MIA. Tickets for two shows had been sold, the return of live music at the Broadway had been heralded in South Jersey newspapers and now Platt was faced with pulling the plug on the show.

"My heart was in my mouth," Platt recalled. "People think all you have to do is unlock the front doors and sell tickets. That's the easy part." Adds Fargo: "I was doing a little sweating backstage, I can tell you!" One hour before showtime, Fargo's bus — and the band's gear — finally pulled up on Theatre Avenue. No one applauded louder than Duffy Platt when Donna Fargo, sporting a sequined white jumpsuit emblazoned with the number 1, strode onstage.

"The first big entertainment act to hit Pitman since 1943 had something for everyone," the Pitman Review reported.

"Country western singer Donna Fargo presented a show that touched all musical bases. Fargo could really belt it out with the best of them but her voice seemed better suited for those melodramatic tear-jerking ballads that country music is so famous for."

And back in the balcony for one night only was Al Beckett, who had come out of retirement to run the spotlight for the shows just as he had each Saturday night during the Broadway's vaudeville era. He conceded to a Review reporter that the Broadway — and show business — were in his blood. Pointing to the Kimball organ down front, he reflected on the silent-film era of his youth: "Each theatre had a personality which was expressed by the organist. They could make or break pictures." Beckett then spotted some familiar faces below. "They all know me," Beckett said, waving to the Pitmanites packing in for the second show. With a twinkle in his eye, he added, "They're all asking, 'Is that old bastard still around?'" The evening would serve as Beckett's final curtain call at the theatre he loved and worked in for nearly half a century. He would die three years later at age 73.

Having a packed house for two shows on a Friday night was an intoxicating new experience for Duffy Platt. He wanted another hit. With Donna Fargo's tour bus now due at Carnegie Hall, Platt immediately rebooked her for another set of shows. Recalls Fargo: "We agreed to come back because Mr. Platt was so great. He was always so appreciative. Back then things were different. Country people appreciated the country artists coming to them where they were in their communities. If they wanted me to, I always stayed after to sign autographs. I appreciated their attention to the music. It was a great relationship."

By February, Platt had begun marketing his lineup of country-western concerts as "Pitman Country." Successful shows featuring Freddy Fender and the Oak Ridge Boys soon followed. And then Don Williams, Roy Clark, Kitty Wells, Hank Snow, Joe Stampley, Crystal Gayle, Billy "Crash" Craddock, Janie Fricke, Marty Robbins, Moe Bandy, the Kendalls, Larry Gatlin, Jeannie C. Riley and Rick Nelson. Before each show, Platt, a self-professed "ham at heart," would stride onstage, his hair slicked back and wearing a sport jacket with boutonniere, to introduce the evening's entertainment. Backstage, he had a photographer ready to document him with the famous country performers he was bringing to town.

But Platt wasn't the only starstruck Pitmanite. Michael Razze Jr. was a kid living on West Jersey Avenue in the 1970s. "When those big buses came into town with Conway Twitty or Mel Tillis, all of us kids would scurry down to Theatre Avenue to see these famous people get off the bus," Razze recalls. "The stars would wave to us. As a kid, it made Pitman feel special to me."

The Pitman Country concert series was attracting repeat customers, with about 100 regulars coming back for each show, many wanting to sit in the same seats. Ralph J. Richards Jr. and his wife, Marcia, sat in the second row just behind Duffy Platt's mother, Mildred. "I didn't like going into Philly for shows and this was right down the street," says Ralph Richards. "We loved seeing these big names right here in Pitman." As a favor to Platt, Richards would take a poster for each show and hang it up at his job at Texaco to promote the concerts. Afterward, he tossed them into a pile. "By the end, I must have had a stack of 50 of the Broadway country posters." Ralph and Marcia's favorites remain in frames, many with saved ticket stubs, hanging on the walls of their basement.

Pitman's friendly small-town aesthetics were perfect for country stars with a hankering for home. Freddy Fender, for example, sat on the stage and signed autographs and kissed female fans until 1:30 in the morning.

While former teen idol Rick Nelson (who had scored a comeback hit in 1972 with "Garden Party") attracted a college crowd, Platt described the audience for Johnny Paycheck (the singer behind the blue-collar anthem "Take This Job and Shove It") as "scrungy." In order to make the numbers work in his 1,200-seat theatre, Platt focused on volume. His live-performance business plan was simple — if he kept ticket prices low and booked each act to do back-to-back shows at 8 and 10 p.m., he could make enough to pay the talent. Donna Fargo set you back $7 for the main floor or $6 for the balcony. Tom T. Hall was $10 and $8. Charley Pride was $15 and $14. While Platt was often cagey about discussing exact numbers with reporters ("My accountant wouldn't like that"), he conceded he was just breaking even on some shows.

Like the vaudeville performers before them, many of the country artists played the Broadway because it was a good-paying gig in a previously untapped Northeastern market adjacent to bigger venues. But for Duffy Platt's next big country booking, Tammy Wynette, Pitman felt like home.

And the First Lady of Country's connection to South Jersey would grow even deeper after she suddenly collapsed backstage at the Broadway and had to be rushed to Underwood Memorial Hospital.

Owner Clayton "Duffy" Platt with country performer Kitty Wells.
Backstage at the Broadway Theatre, 1981.
Photo by Charles W. Walker Jr. Courtesy of Daniel Munyon.

CHAPTER SEVEN

"C.E. Platt Exclusive Producer Brings You Tammy Wynette On Stage Live!"
1978–1982

Clayton Platt knew he was doing something right with the Pitman Country concert series when a Philadelphia Inquirer reporter and a photographer drove across the Walt Whitman bridge into South Jersey to interview him over a grilled cheese sandwich. Later dubbing Pitman "Nashville North" in his article, the Inquirer reporter seated across from Platt at the Pitman Restaurant wanted to know how he'd gotten away with charging $21 a head to see "Hee-Haw" star Roy Clark. In his feature story, Inky reporter Al Haas wrote, "It prompted a mild buzz in rural, intimate Pitman (population, 10,257), where folks figured that Platt had obtained a permit to print money."

Platt's name-brand bookings in Pitman had also elicited wonder — and a bit of jealousy — from his bigger competitors across the bridge. After all, a Merle Haggard show at Philly's Tower Theatre had been canceled when the country star couldn't draw enough local fans to make the show profitable. A Lynn Anderson concert at the Academy of Music had been similarly scrapped. Wrote Haas: "Everyone in the business knows that country music does not draw in large Northeast metropolitan areas like New York and Philadelphia."

"I knew it would draw attention," Platt said simply of the $21 ticket price for Roy Clark, between bites of sandwich, taking a breather from one of the five cigars he had stashed in the breast pocket of his blue quilted hunting vest. "When I went down to Nashville recently, they didn't know me. But they did know about the guy who charged $21 to see Roy Clark."

While Roy Clark was the most expensive, the fastest-selling show in Pitman Country history was Tammy Wynette's debut at the Broadway on March 31, 1978. All seats were reserved, with the orchestra costing $10, the mezzanine $9 and the balcony $8. Platt sold out two shows and promptly rebooked the country queen. But Wynette's return visit to Pitman on a bill with singer-songwriter Whisperin' Bill Anderson on March 30, 1979, proved more dramatic. Coming offstage following her second show, Wynette collapsed. She was admitted to the intensive care unit at Underwood Memorial Hospital in Woodbury, diagnosed with peritonitis. She remained at Underwood under 24-hour guard for a week. "That should discourage fans from visiting her," husband and manager George Richey told the Daily Times. Pitman Country regular Ralph Richards Jr. was more than a little acquainted with one of the security guards posted outside Wynette's hospital room. It was his stepfather, Albert Quinlan. "He worked security at Underwood Memorial as a part-time job," explains

Richards. "He never said a word about it until after she was discharged."

In the years that followed, Wynette's hospital stays would become more frequent. Her friend and future fellow Broadway Theatre performer Loretta Lynn remembered one night Tammy was hospitalized in Atlanta while Lynn was playing a show in Macon. "I heard a knock on the hotel room door around 1:30 in the morning," Lynn recalled in 2002. "I looked through the peephole and said, 'That sure as heck looks like Tammy Wynette out there in a housecoat.' She had escaped and gotten her a pilot to fly her down to Macon! I said, 'Tammy, you're gonna get caught.' She said, 'Shoot, I'll be back in that bed by daylight. They'll never know.' We sat up all night gossiping about George Jones."

In September, booked to perform at the Valley Forge Music Fair in Devon, Pennsylvania, Wynette was once again taken to Underwood Hospital, this time for a hernia operation. Wynette made the unusual interstate transportation request because of the care she had received at Underwood earlier in the year. The country icon loved performing in Pitman at the Broadway and returned twice in 1980 and again in 1982.

But it was her fall 1980 appearance with ex-husband George Jones, then known as "No-Show Jones" for his habit of getting drunk and blowing off concerts, that was of particular interest to Pitman Country fans. "We're the Sonny and Cher of country music," Wynette explained. By 1980, Jones, facing bankruptcy due to $1.5 million in debt associated with 54 canceled concert dates, clearly needed the reunion tour with his former spouse. Asked to recount the reason for the pair's 1975 divorce, Wynette was succinct: "My naggin' and his nippin'."

"Tammy was probably the most popular out of all the country stars who played the Broadway," remembers Joan Schaeffer Eldredge, who attended many Pitman Country shows with her husband, Ralph, her sister Barbara and brother-in-law Lee. Growing up, Joan, Barbara and their younger sister Betty Lou had lived over Al's Television Service, their father Al Schaeffer Jr.'s TV and radio repair business on West Jersey Avenue across from the train station. "I worked in the finishing department at CBS Records in Pitman," Joan says. "Tammy was signed to [CBS affiliate label] Epic Records, so lots of her albums were pressed at the Pitman plant. Tammy just had a way of relating to the Pitman crowd. I think it was because we were small-town people

Barbara Mandrell greeting fans in Pitman.
Photo by Charles W. Walker Jr. Courtesy of Daniel Munyon.

like she was. She understood us. People were surprised by how popular the Broadway country shows were. But I knew, because I was seeing all of those country albums come down the line each day. If we were pressing them, that meant somebody was buying them."

Platt was ever the showman and his Pitman Country newspaper ads now included "C.E. Platt Exclusive Producer Brings You ..." at the top. And in dealings with the press, Platt dusted off a few of the skills he had acquired onstage as a drama student at Glassboro High. On the phone with a booking agent as a Courier-Post reporter sat a few feet away, Platt peered over his reading glasses, cigar dangling from his mouth. He objected to an exorbitant appearance fee being floated by saying, "I don't want him anyway!" and hanging up. "We're getting calls from agencies that didn't want to talk to us before," he explained. While Roy Clark remained a personal favorite, Platt still liked to complain about the skyrocketing costs of booking the "Hee-Haw" star. "We had Roy in September 1978 and he cost us $25,000 and now he's charging us $50,000. The popularity of these groups has gone up. And if they win awards, forget it. The Mandrell Sisters, now that they have a TV show, you can't even touch them." By 1981, Platt had built a mailing list of 10,000 Pitman Country patrons from New York to Virginia.

By 1980, in addition to country, Platt was booking other acts on the Broadway stage, including legendary comic Henny Youngman, Judy Collins, Dr. Hook, Helen Reddy, Air Supply, The Lettermen and a 1950s night with Danny and the Juniors, The Shirelles and The Dovells. He also flirted with the idea of booking Talking Heads. Ultimately, Platt couldn't strike a deal with the emerging new-wave rock group. "I guess they were out looking for another head," he explained. "They went on tour in Europe."

Back in his cramped office, Platt reprised his country music impresario routine for the entertainment editor of the Gloucester County Times. "Tell me the dates you have open for Mickey Gilley," asked Platt on a call with a William Morris agent, exhaling a cloud of cigar smoke. "August 14? Ah, too bad, we have Charley Pride in here that night." In his story, reporter John Scanlon described his surroundings thusly: "[Platt's] office would make Felix Unger cry. It's a shoebox cluttered with trade publications, concert posters, correspondence from talent agents. Paperwork is tacked on the walls, piled on his desk, stacked in chairs."

As a newly minted music mogul, Platt was also having to deal with the headaches of artist riders in contracts.

Pianist and singer-songwriter Leon Russell's contract, for example, represented a particular throbbing migraine for the theatre owner. For starters, 144 peeled jumbo shrimp plus cocktail sauce were required in the green room upon Russell's arrival. The performer was also requesting, in no particular order: two cases of Perrier water, chilled; 2 gallons of Mountain Valley spring water, chilled; a half-gallon of Ocean Spray cranberry juice; a case of Michelob; assorted raw vegetables and Townhouse or Ritz crackers — plus hot meals for 15, including a selection of vegetarian dishes. "Some of their requests are ridiculous," groused Platt to the Gloucester County Times. "They buckle their pants the same as I do. I like shrimp but I don't eat it before I introduce an act. I don't make ice cubes out of spring water." Platt also had to find space to park Russell's 60-foot bus, two limousines, motor home and 1-ton van.

"Fernwood 2 Night" star and standup comic Martin Mull, meanwhile, required thrift shop furniture. "I've got to find an old couch for Mull," Platt explained. "That's what it says in his [contract] rider, he needs a tacky living room set."

Illusionist The Amazing Kreskin required a cot to lie on "for 45 minutes to rest and concentrate" between shows, plus fresh fruit, peanut butter and crackers. "You know, that son of a gun took it all with him," said Platt. "Larry Gatlin didn't even eat all of the sandwiches we brought in. And he didn't open the jar of honey. But what the hell, I had a sold-out house. Don Williams carries this old coffee pot. He sets it up in his dressing room and you never see him. They just sat down there, playing jazz and drinking coffee."

Across the street from the theatre, the owners of the Pit-man Restaurant were only too happy to accommodate the late-night hours of hungry country stars, who were quickly supplying the walls with autographed 8-by-10s. In 1978, Tammy Wynette and husband George Richey walked in famished after she finished a pair of shows. By 4 a.m., Richey had wolfed down seven cheese steaks — with hot peppers. "They pay for everything," Helen Wuerthner, who with husband Fred owned and ran the restaurant, told the Times. "They just appreciate us opening for them because they're so tired of the quick stops. They're just down-to-earth people who really appreciate what you do." The artist formerly known as Ricky Nelson on "The Adventures of Ozzie and Harriet" sitcom, meanwhile, spied a guitar left in a corner of the restaurant by Helen and Fred's daughter Dawn and offered her a few lessons. "We couldn't believe it," said Fred. "I even talked to Roy Clark in his dressing room. Well, when I got back to the restaurant, I was good for nothing."

But unlike Platt's popular country concerts, not all of his live bookings were welcomed by Pitmanites. Church groups immediately mobilized when Platt announced his July 1979 weeklong engagement of "Here It Is, Burlesque!" starring veteran striptease artist Ann Corio, who had famously lent her name to the 1962 LP "How to Strip For Your Husband." Joining her onstage were former vaudeville comic Pinky Lee and emcee and fellow vaudeville vet Morey Amsterdam (best known for playing gag writer Buddy Sorrell on "The Dick Van Dyke Show") and a male stripper, Patrick Bagwell.

Morey Amsterdam and Ann Corio in "Here It Is, Burlesque!" in 1979.

Photo courtesy of Daniel Munyon.

Upset residents went to the borough council armed with petitions to stop the show. Clayton Platt himself showed up to assure officials the show, which had already made stops in Fort Worth, Cleveland and Cincinnati on its national tour, would not feature bare breasts or male frontal nudity. With Platt's notoriety for playing X-rated films, some residents were not reassured.

For days, headlines swirled until town officials tentatively decided Platt could move forward with the week of shows being filmed at the Broadway as a 90-minute HBO special. When

"Here It Is, Burlesque!" made its cable debut in the fall of 1979, producers used local headlines generated by the controversy to open the show.

In an interview with the Courier-Post, Ann Corio sounded more like one of Pitman's concerned citizens than one of the world's most famous striptease artists. "Not everyone knows the difference between naughty and vulgar. The public is saturated by total nudity and four-letter words." Against the backdrop of the more explicit entertainment of the late 1970s, Corio argued the times were perfect for the reintroduction of an art form from a more innocent era. Pinky Lee added, "I don't go for vulgarity. I do one scene [in 'Here It Is, Burlesque!'] where two girls are seducing me. The theme is provocative, but it's done cutely."

Covering the show's opening night at the Broadway, the Courier-Post wrote:

"Petitions from some residents to add 'cover' to the show all seemed forgotten the moment Miss Corio's eight dancers stepped out in pink Victorian costumes more than abbreviated for the period. Poking fun at any protest — and indeed, welcoming it for its publicity value — Morey Amsterdam told the crowd, 'I'll make every street in Pitman a one-way heading south and let Glassboro worry about it.' While Tammy Roche's wriggling in a see-through champagne bath was cleanly provocative and the corps boldly got down to pasties and G-string, no one violated Miss Corio's 'naughty but never vulgar' promise."

Also in the audience on opening night? Pitman solicitor Warren Carr. After receiving petitions, the borough council had sent its lawyer to the show to report back on whether it was lewd. In a letter to council afterward, Carr stated that while parts of the show were "suggestive," he did not believe it would be legally possible to obtain an injunction against the performances. In order to violate federal and state laws, he explained, the performance must be "blatantly lewd and lascivious." The show, in his opinion, was neither. On the contrary, Carr wrote, he found the show "lively and interesting." Over 45 years later, Carr reflects that the outing was not among the worst tasks the borough ever assigned to him. "I was going to sit in the back and hide," Carr recalls. "But when I showed up, there was somebody waiting to ambush me. They gave me a seat way down front. Later, the local newspaper described my attendance, comparing it to sending a fox into the henhouse."

"My wife wasn't happy about it, but I got us tickets," reflects Ralph Richards with a laugh. "It turned out to be a great show." Richards still has the orange, yellow and green-hued "'Here It Is, Burlesque!' Live On Stage — 10 Beautiful Girls Direct From Las Vegas" poster, complete with the couple's programs and ticket stubs preserved under glass and hanging in their basement. The show was such a hit, Clayton Platt brought it back to the Broadway in the summer of 1980 for another successful run — this time without petitions or protests.

In between controversial burlesque show bookings, the Broadway's movie crowds continued to dwindle for screenings of R-rated film fare of the era, including "The Amityville Horror" and "Halloween." As a result, Duffy Platt had a reputation among the kids in town for not squinting too closely at the ages of his remaining patrons. Carmen Cattafi, who lived on the street behind the theatre, says he recalls seeing the raunchy John Belushi college comedy

"National Lampoon's Animal House" and "Cheech and Chong's Next Movie," both rated R, when he was 11 or 12. "It was a dollar and we were always let in, regardless of rating

Photo courtesy of Daniel Munyon.

or whether we had an adult with us," remembers Cattafi. "Duffy Platt would also do a special Halloween show where he would show old Vincent Price horror movies like 'The Conqueror Worm' and all the kids in town would pile in and scream our heads off. It was just for us to have a good time."

Platt also potentially traumatized a generation of kids when he showed writer-director George A. Romero's "Dawn of the Dead" at the Broadway, the long-awaited sequel to Romero's trailblazing 1968 zombie cult classic "Night of the Living Dead." The 1979 film was so violent and gore-filled, it was unrated. In his review, film critic Roger

Ebert described the film as "gruesome, sickening, disgusting, brutal and appalling" as well as "one of the best horror films ever made." Ironically, given the financial havoc the Deptford Mall was wreaking on the Broadway and Pitman's business district at the time, the entire blood-soaked satire of American consumerism took place inside a deserted mall. Pitman resident Ray Biddle was 13 at the time and got into the movie thanks to "Dog," the older brother of his ball hockey teammate. Remembers Biddle: "It was scary as hell, but I love zombie movies to this day." Perhaps not coincidentally, Biddle would grow up to write, direct and produce independent zombie pictures.

One night of the year that always guaranteed Platt a capacity crowd? On July 3, at 7:45 p.m. sharp, the town would turn out at the Broadway for the annual Miss Pitman pageant. The high school competition had started in 1955 as part of the town's 50th anniversary celebration, with "Waterfront" star Preston Foster crowning Lois Haight. The second Miss Pitman contest was held in Ballard Park in 1960; the Sunset Auditorium would also host the event.

But it was a particularly sweltering night inside the Pitman Masonic hall in 1974 that inspired a permanent venue change for the pageant. Contestant Sue Lanning Crispin remembers the evening well. "It was packed in the Masonic hall and there was no air conditioning." Lanning ended up winning the coveted Miss Pitman crown that night. "There was a picture in the paper the next day and my hair was completely frizzed out!" she recalls, laughing. "We were certainly glad to get into the air-conditioned Broadway Theatre the next year." In 1975, Lanning would hand off her crown onstage at the Broadway and play the theatre's prized Kimball organ as well. The Broadway would serve as the pageant's home for the next 20 years.

Contestants were judged on talent, evening gown, poise and personality. Various civic organizations and businesses sponsored the high school students. For decades, Pitman insurance agent Joe Dargan was the pageant's beloved emcee. Almost every year, at one point during the three-hour pageant, would point to the Broadway's signature boxes and deadpan, "Be careful up there, that's how Lincoln got it!" Existing camcorder

Miss Pitman pageant emcee Joe Dargan onstage at the Broadway Theatre, 1986.

footage from the 1986 pageant highlights the talent competition and a rousing Rockettes-inspired routine from the town's Corrine Gangi dancers. As the evening drew to a close, Dargan attempted to calm the amped-up attendees cheering for their classmates. "Settle down, I have a whole lot of things to read here, but I haven't the time to do it. The judges have already made their decision. This is unprecedented!"

Ripping a hole in the side of the envelope, Dargan added, "I must caution our winner I'm probably tearing your $100 check in half. You'll also get a trophy, but the check is worth more!" In 1986, Amy Lynn Gruber won both Miss Congeniality and the Miss Pitman title.

Miss Pitman 1974 Sue Lanning Crispin has gone on to become the pageant's director, guiding two generations of high school women down the runway. "Since 1955, we've all been a part of the same tradition," she says. "It's a platform and a stepping-stone to develop and display your talents." Many contestants have gone on to build successful resumes, including Miss Pitman 2010, Madeline Brewer. The Emmy-nominated actress now stars in "The Handmaid's Tale," playing Janine Lindo.

Tammy DeLucas Razze, who competed in the 1988 competition, still has fond memories of her evening onstage at the Broadway. She had just started dating her now-husband, Michael L. Razze Jr., who was seated in a box. Since she took dance lessons at Corrine Gangi's studio in Pitman, DeLucas tap danced to Barry Manilow's "Jump Shout Boogie." Recalls DeLucas Razze: "Back then, I was really shy. But I definitely think being in all those dance recitals gave me confidence. The pageant was a big deal because it was held at the Broadway. It was nerve-wracking being up there in the heart of the community on that historic stage."

The next day, in the July 4th parade outside on Broadway, all of the Miss Pitman contestants waved to the crowd as they rolled down the street perched atop convertibles, a tradition that continues to this day. "To have that many people come out to Miss Pitman on the night before the parade is just what you did," recalls Michael Razze Jr. "You knew everyone who was in it and their families and the people sponsoring them."

In 1994, the Miss Pitman pageant moved to the newly constructed auditorium at Pitman High. But the pageant occasionally finds its way back to the Broadway, as it did for the pageant's 60th anniversary in 2015, which featured an array of former Miss Pitmans in their crowns. Adding to the evening's sense of history, Domenica Granato Castro, the daughter of Miss Pitman 1980, Suzanne Granato Castro, was crowned Miss Pitman 2015.

Up in the Broadway's projection booth, some of the new staffers lacked the technical aptitude Al Beckett had displayed for decades. In the summer of 1982, 20-year-old Glassboro State film major Ken Paul Rosenthal was hired as a projectionist. During a screening of the Steven Spielberg-produced supernatural hit "Poltergeist," Rosenthal accidentally plunged the theatre into darkness when he failed to turn on a projector light to illuminate the film's next reel. And then there was the evening he accidentally set a print of the teen sex comedy "Porky's" afire when he turned the projector light on but failed to engage the motor to move the movie through the machine. "I just remember watching the film melt on the screen, like a hippie art film," recounts Rosenthal, who is now an indie filmmaker. He vividly recalls what happened next: Duffy Platt flew up the stairs and into the booth, yanked the burning film out of the projector, rethreaded it and had it back up on screen within seconds.

Rosenthal admits he was better suited to operating the spotlight for Platt's final flurry of big-name country acts booked that summer. For a college kid who had Styx and Foreigner on his turntable, working the spotlight for two of the final concerts proved transformational. After years of trying, Platt had finally secured Loretta Lynn for four shows. Lynn was once again a hot live commodity, thanks to the popularity of her bio pic "Coal Miner's Daughter."

And at each of the four shows she played over two nights in Pitman, Lynn performed her biggest hits, including many of the songs she wrote about her sometimes stormy marriage to Doolittle Lynn. Songs with titles like "Don't Come Home A-Drinkin' (With Lovin' On Your Mind)" and "You Ain't Woman Enough (To Take My Man)." "I was just writin' about what I was goin' through," Lynn reflected in 2008. "What made those songs hits is that other women were goin' through the same things. But back then, women just didn't talk about such things. Songs about cheatin' have always done me right. Now, Doo, he didn't like some of those songs, but Doo ended up making us a lot of money over the years!"

Most memorable for Rosenthal was working the spot for Johnny Cash and wife June Carter Cash's appearance. "This was before his [1990s "American Recordings" album series] career renaissance," remembers Rosenthal. "I was a real music idiot at the time, still listening to Boston and thinking, 'Here come these old fogey country acts.' But when Johnny and June walked out on that stage, I was stunned. I was so moved by that concert I went backstage afterward and picked up a guitar string off the floor and kept it. It was thrilling."

According to Cash's signed American Federation of Musicians contract for the Broadway show, Platt paid Johnny and June $8,750 for two shows. But based on what transpired during sound check that night, it's a wonder the concerts ever went on at all. Onstage strumming his guitar at sound check, Cash happened to glance up. When he saw the microphones dangling above, he immediately grew suspicious. The Man in Black followed the wires running from over the stage up to a cluttered office. That's where Cash and his road manager discovered Clayton Platt's secret taping system that recorded the Pitman Country acts for his private listening pleasure.

For years, various stories have circulated about what happened next. Here's what is known for certain — the evening's 7 o'clock show was delayed. Onstage, Cash explained he needed to have his left knee patched following a bout with a blood clot. And that's the explanation Gloucester County Times entertainment editor John Scanlon later relayed to readers. In his concert review, Scanlon wrote: "'Hi, I'm Johnny Cash,' said The Man in Black, strumming an acoustic guitar as he turned to face the crowd. That's all he had to say, really. Opening with 'Ring of Fire,' Cash moved on to 'Folsom Prison Blues,' aided by video footage of prison scenes projected on a suspended screen. Cash isn't an entertainer tempted by flashy gimmicks. There's simply a swagger to his walk, a crooked arch to his grin. And his coarse, deep-down vocals give the songs a gritty edge. Yet Cash is a gentle man who happily prefers to let his wife and band share the applause."

How gentlemanly Cash and his road manager were with Platt backstage in private remains open to speculation. But Cash and June Carter Cash returned to play their scheduled 9:30 p.m. show.

Somehow, the Broadway's owner had been able to talk his way out of the predicament with Cash. But Clayton Platt would be less successful talking his way out of the lawsuits looming on the horizon. And he had an even more pressing problem — protesters were back. But this time they weren't objecting to porn playing at the Glassboro Theatre.

This time, they were picketing in Pitman, lining the sidewalk outside the Broadway.

*Clayton "Duffy" Platt with singer Rick Nelson, 1979.
Photo by Charles W. Walker Jr. Courtesy of Daniel Munyon.*

CHAPTER EIGHT

"I grew up here, I'm not out to cheat anybody."
1983–2003

The woman standing dejectedly in front of Clayton Platt at the Broadway candy counter was disappointed with the ninth-row tickets he was offering. "You mean I can't get any closer?" she pleaded. Smiling, Platt shook his head and cautioned, "You may not want to get any closer." She sighed, handed him $16 in exchange for two tickets and departed the concession stand. In the winter of 1983, business at the Broadway was once again brisk for Platt's latest booking, the Peter Adonis Traveling Fantasy Show. One customer had just bought a ticket to the all-male strip show for his 70-year-old mother, while other women were creatively shaving $8 off the grocery budget to finance their "Ladies Night Out," as it was being billed.

Like the skirmish between the Broadway and the town four years earlier when he'd brought "Here It Is, Burlesque!" to town, Platt was prepared for blowback. Or as the Gloucester County Times was phrasing it, "jangling the religious nerves and conservative pride that run deep in the small town." Pitman's Ministerium, composed of local church leaders, met to discuss their options. "I think there's always the position one can take that you'll never be able to keep out of the community the kinds of things you don't agree with," reasoned Rev. David Blackburn. "But people at least have the freedom to be able to state that [disagreement]." When the strip show was announced in December, Pitman Mayor Richard Salmon, "representing the moral ears of the community," had approached Platt and requested he not move forward with the show. But unlike a decade earlier, no gentleman's agreement would be reached. Ultimately, Salmon told the Times, there was little the council could do to prevent the show from happening. "I'm not going," he added tersely.

In its preview of the show, the Gloucester County Times described the act as "the Village People of strip — dancers in macho costumes take them off for women of all ages who want to kiss them, hug them and even tuck dollar bills into their G-strings." Of the troupe's appeal, a dancer known onstage as Joe Goodnight explained, "We're not the best-looking guys in the world. But I think the way we bring it across is what makes it work. My theory is if you get the women laughing, you break down the inhibitions."

The 400 people outside the Broadway picketing with "No Sodom & Gomorrah in Pitman" signs on Feb. 3, 1983, weren't laughing.

"Why should a woman come look at a man take off his clothes?" asked protester Hank LaBor, clutching a Bible as he marched. "She can stay home and watch her husband do that." Added the Rev. George Eisenhart of the Lambs Road

Assembly of God Church, shouting through a bullhorn: "You can love your lust, but we don't want it!" One demonstrator carried a sign reading, "Sin Destroys the Home," while another invoked the namesake of the borough: "The Bones of Rev. Pitman Say Resist." Reported the Camden Courier-Post: "The onlookers included one amazed storekeeper who said she recognized a shoplifter in the parade."

Fourth-generation Pitmanite Jane McCausland was among the sea of protesters out on Broadway that night. "Most of the churches in town were out there marching," she remembers. "For us, it was about protecting town values. Pitman was started as a Methodist summer camp and this was totally against what the founding fathers envisioned for the town. It was not something that aligned with the morals of Pitman."

Arriving early, many protesters purposely parked on Broadway to inconvenience show attendees. But some of the women excitedly rushing in to see the show stopped long enough under the "Ladies Night Out" marquee to defiantly wave their tickets at the protesters before dashing inside. Other attendees had made signs to counter the protesters. They grinned for newspaper photographers as they held their "Adam Wore Only a Fig Leaf in the Garden" and "I Don't Picket Your Church, Don't Picket Our Theatre" signage.

Inside the Broadway, the women-only crowd (save for two male security guards posted down front) "clapped and cheered itself into a frenzy at the first sight of the jiggling beefcake," according to the Courier-Post. Some attendees used binoculars to ogle the men onstage, while others brought along cameras to document the evening's entertainment. "We come to see them wherever we find them," explained Winnie Steinmetz, 60, of Atlantic City, attending with her 29-year-old daughter. The Courier-Post observed, "the women streaming into the plush bordello-red interior of the Broadway Theatre were oblivious to prayers, hymns or the possible corruption of their souls."

Among the celebrants inside? Bobbi Wilkins, the former granddaughter-in-law of the Broadway's original owner, out on the town with girlfriends, the wife of an NFL quarterback and a staffer at a faith-based nonprofit. They were hiding behind her to avoid the news cameras. "I couldn't figure out what the big deal was," Wilkins recalls, laughing. "It was scandalous. People were asking, 'What are they doing in Pitman?!'"

Ticket stubs from the Pitman Country music series. Pitman Historical Museum.

Standing in the back of the theatre, Duffy Platt was beaming. TV news crews from all three Philadelphia stations were inside the Broadway, shooting footage for their 11 p.m. newscasts. Platt had sold out the male strip show in a week and was already busy inking a deal to bring the group back. But a few hundred yards down Broadway at Pitman United Methodist Church, parishioners were busy holding a prayer service and signing a petition to deliver to the borough council urging that "adult book stores, X-rated movies and other X-rated performances" be banned in the borough. "Christian rights have been trampled," protest organizer Ruth Hopkins told the Gloucester County Times. "This is going to serve as notice that we are going to stand up for our rights."

From his perspective, Platt saw nothing wrong with the Peter Adonis Fantasy Show. "Look, I brought everybody in town together. We're not out to lower the standards of the community. And by the way, tickets are selling, there are people out there who want to see this show. They play supper clubs all over the country. I'm not here to ruin this town. We've got a religious program coming in next, a barbershop music group and Wolfman Jack coming in to do a '50s show. Who knows what's next? Maybe it'll be female mud wrestling."

By the time the male strippers returned to the Broadway stage in April, the borough had passed a new ordinance banning pornography in Pitman (the ordinance, notably, did not apply to the titillating-but-G-string-secured show in question). At April's Peter Adonis show, the only protesting pastor was onstage. "The Rev. U.R. Profit" scolded, "Shame on you women, right here in Pitman!" before promptly shedding his priestly attire. In the audience, 71-year-old attendee Mary Crawn told the Times, "Don't let them fool you, there's a lot of church people here." Down the street at Broadway and Holly Avenue, members of the Methodist Church were holding an alternative Ladies Night Out — a ham dinner served by male church members with a performance by the local singing group Gospel Magic. "We view it as an alternative to what's going on down the street," explained organizer Ruth Hopkins.

While Duffy Platt was all smiles in front of the TV cameras filming his sold-out strip shows, privately, he was two years behind on paying his property taxes. Consequently, in May 1984, the Pitman borough council voted unanimously to begin foreclosure proceedings against the Broadway Theatre. Pitman solicitor Warren Carr explained to the *Times* that Platt had reneged on a monthly repayment plan he had made with council officials. He now owed more than $10,000 in back taxes. Due to financial hard times in Pitman's business district (many shoppers now preferred Deptford Mall), the borough was dealing with more than $284,000 in delinquent tax payments. "That rate of delinquencies was highly unusual," recounts Carr. "But the mall had literally killed Woodbury [the county seat of South Jersey's Gloucester County] and it certainly had a deep impact on businesses in Pitman."

By August, Duffy Platt's legal woes had worsened when the New Jersey attorney general filed suit, charging him with violating the state's anti-scalping and consumer fraud statutes. The charges stemmed from a series of canceled concerts at the Broadway. Instead of offering refunds to patrons, Platt had tried to stem his financial bleeding by re-booking the shows, often in vain. Platt would later complain to *The Philadelphia Inquirer* that some acts like Rick Nelson canceled more than once. "You have four people cancel on you and you're down the tubes," he said. "That's what happened to us."

Pitman native Debra Moore Higbee was among those who had waited patiently for months for her $160 refund on four tickets from a canceled show. After months of hearing excuses, Higbee showed up one night to confront Duffy Platt's girlfriend Delores Wernick, who was working the concession stand. "When it was my turn in line, I explained who I was and that I wanted my refund," recalls Higbee. "I was told, 'Oh, we'll send it to you,' and I told her, 'No, I've heard that for months and now you're going to give me back my money.' She said, 'Either you get out of line or I'm calling the police.' I told her, 'Great, that's exactly who I want you to call because I will tell them you've defrauded me.'" Wernick counted out $160 from the concession cash register and handed it to Higbee.

Meanwhile, 175 other Broadway regulars were banding together to file suit against the theatre owner, seeking more than $7,000 in refunds. Bill Anderson and other performers, including T.G. Sheppard, had also filed suit against Platt. In all, he was now staring down half a dozen lawsuits and impending foreclosure.

Finally, in November 1984, after a two-and-a-half-hour negotiation, Platt's attorney Joseph Lisa and Deputy Attorney General Phyllis Forsyth reached a settlement. The deal was cut just 48 hours before Platt was to stand trial. The state was seeking to permanently restrain him from selling tickets, a move that would have effectively put the theatre owner out of business. The settlement dictated that Platt refund Broadway patrons $7,049 through the state Division of Consumer Affairs and pay $2,000 to the state for administrative fees and $500 in court costs. "The order," stated attorney Lisa, "specifically does not contain any admission or finding of guilt." The deal also called for Platt to make monthly installments to the state Consumer Affairs office over a seven-month period.

The settlement with the state did nothing to stave off Platt's now-$12,000 tax trouble with the town. As a result, in the Dec. 9, 1984, edition of the Gloucester County Times, a public notice announced Pitman tax collector Lois C. Thompson would hold a public auction at 2 p.m. on Dec. 18, 1984, to sell the Broadway Theatre to the highest bidder. With no bids at the auction, the Borough of Pitman assumed title to the 1926 landmark. Meanwhile, instead of adhering to the state's schedule of repayment as outlined in the deal with the attorney general's office, Platt decided to dispute the agreed-to administrative costs. In November 1985, in trouble with the state for reneging on the settlement and the borough – where he now owed $25,000 in back taxes – Platt filed for reorganization under federal bankruptcy laws. Among the creditors listed were performers T.G. Sheppard; Whisperin' Bill Anderson; and the New York law firm Sargoy, Stein & Hanft, representing multiple film distribution companies seeking $11,700 for films rented to Platt for exhibition he hadn't paid for.

Platt's lawyers filed the bankruptcy to head off the theatre's foreclosure by the borough, now desperate for its $25,000 in back taxes during a financially fraught time for the town. On the timing of the bankruptcy filing, Pitman solicitor Warren Carr explained to the Times, "We can't get the title to the property now" since the filing froze the process. "When and if the theatre is sold, they have to pay us off first." Pitman's tax collector, Lois Thompson, told the newspaper the town had been especially lenient with Platt, considering "he had failed to pay any of the owed taxes under the arrangement worked out in 1983." But the borough also recognized the optics of having the town's most recognized business, located in the center of its commercial district, vacant and boarded up.

The Broadway's bankruptcy became the Dec. 22, 1985, cover story of The Philadelphia Inquirer's South Jersey Neighbors section. In the feature, Platt, now 55, opened up to reporter Kitty Dumas during an interview at the theatre. Dumas described her surroundings to readers: "Dust clings to the crystal chandeliers, there's peeling wallpaper and paint and the musty scent of age and wear and neglect is everywhere."

"I grew up here," Platt said. "I'm not out to cheat anybody. If I was, I would have left town." He added defiantly, "I'm still here and we're still open." Platt also discussed the realities of attempting to operate a single-screen theatre in an **aging** 1926 movie house, surrounded by the now-14-screen Deptford Mall Cinema in the age of home video. Departing the theatre, Dumas noted the current attraction playing: Charles Bronson's "Death Wish 2."

In order to financially keep his head above water, a requirement of his reorganization filing, Platt began renting the Broadway to the interdenominational Gloucester County Community Church for Sunday services. Regrettably, in an attempt to spruce up the theatre's downstairs, church members unknowingly painted over 60 years of history — the accumulated vaudeville and other performer autographs on the dressing room and green room walls.

Never one to shy away from controversy, Duffy Platt booked director Martin Scorsese's sprawling biblical epic "The Last Temptation of Christ" for Thanksgiving week 1988. The film reimagines the Christ story, granting the son of God a last-minute reprieve on the cross with the help of a guardian angel. Jesus goes on to marry Mary Magdalene (notably consummating their marriage) and living into old age. Mother Angelica, a Catholic nun, described the film as "the most blasphemous ridicule of the Eucharist that's ever been perpetuated in this world … a movie that has the power to destroy souls eternally." In nearby Pennsville, N.J., bowing to public outcry, the owner of the Penn Twin Theatre vowed the movie "will not ever be shown here." In contrast, Platt, seeing paying customers pouring in, gladly held the film over into the first week of December.

The theatre owner was also getting some much-needed help. A recent transplant to Cedar Avenue, resident Daniel Munyon was fascinated by the town's historic movie house. He introduced himself to Platt after taking in a film one night in 1990. "Munyon, Munyon," Platt replied, rolling the name around in his memory. "Do you have an aunt named Gloria?" Munyon nodded. Platt grimaced and said, "I loved

Uptown Pitman, early 1980s. From the author's collection.

that woman, but she went back to her husband. I never forgave her for that." After further comparing familial notes, Dan Munyon discovered that Duffy Platt was his sister's godfather. With the ice broken, Munyon told Platt that if he ever considered selling the Broadway, he'd gladly take it off his hands. Platt shook his head. Munyon then asked if he could have a job at the Broadway. Platt again shook his head. Then he added, "You can volunteer if you want." Munyon recalls, "The theatre business wasn't a joke to him. He was there to make money, end of conversation. He put as little money into that building as he had to. Aside from going to dinner with his girlfriend, Delores, if the lights were on, Mr. Platt was at the theatre, working."

In fall 1992, help for the Broadway's peeling paint and crumbling plaster arrived in the form of theatre restorer George Grady and his assistant John Durham. Grady, who had also worked on restoring the Count Basie Theatre in Red Bank, N.J., specialized in historically accurate work. Climbing a long ladder to reach the theatre's intricate ceiling designs, Grady examined the multiple spots where falling plaster had been replaced by mold. The pair used turkey feathers as paintbrushes to "marbleize" the theatre's walls. Grady also hauled in a huge mixing tub to apply plaster to the Broadway's aging walls. "Everything's intact, the way it was," Grady told a Gloucester County Times reporter, gesturing from the Broadway balcony. He added hopefully, "Deterioration has been taking over but we're here to stop that."

Beginning in 1994, volunteers from the Southern Jersey chapter of the American Theatre Organ Society dutifully arrived early each Saturday morning to work on the venue's vintage Kimball organ. The instrument was in desperate need of maintenance nearly 70 years after its installation. When the group first encountered the Kimball, it was virtually unplayable. "The more you dug into it, the worse it became," said Joe Rementer, a member of the SJ-ATOS restoration team. Once a week the volunteer group met and slowly took the Kimball apart piece by piece to replace or repair nonworking parts, clean others and then carefully reinstall them. The restoration would ultimately take eight years. That same year, by the time the Keanu Reeves and Sandra Bullock action movie "Speed" arrived on screen at the Broadway, Clayton Platt had found the money to install Dolby Stereo and Digital Theatre Sound at the Broadway.

Meanwhile, the theatre's most dedicated volunteer, Dan Munyon, was seeking a change in status. He again asked Platt if he could purchase the Broadway from him. Platt again said no but offered to strike a deal with Munyon — come to work at the Broadway, learn the business from him and then he'd sell him the theatre. Munyon agreed and became Platt's shadow around the place. "When he went up to the shack on the roof to deal with the air conditioning, I was up there watching what they did," Munyon remembers. "I stood in the ticket booth and watched. I learned projection and how to set up the stage. I listened to everything he was talking about on the phone. I wanted to learn everything I could from him."

By the summer of 1996, having Munyon in place at the Broadway was fortuitous for Platt since he was now embroiled in another scandal in Glassboro. In his capacity as highway administrator, Platt had been accused by the Glassboro borough council "of abusing his position using highway department employees, equipment and supplies in two businesses [an excavation firm and a construction business] he privately co-owned." Platt was also accused of purchasing two Australian oak desks and bookshelves "at a $12,000 cost to taxpayers." Meanwhile, Gloucester County Times sources verified that the sales agent for the furniture company was Delores Wernick, "Platt's live-in girlfriend." Platt denied the allegations.

A defiant Platt continued to show up to work at the Glassboro Highway Department. In response, the town highway committee voted unanimously to suspend him. Pending the outcome of a borough investigation and an indictment decision from the Gloucester County prosecutor's office, the borough took away Platt's company truck and changed the locks on his office door. Adding to the mounting pressure, the Times ran an editorial in its Nov. 21, 1996, edition demanding Platt be fired after a grand jury declined to charge him with a crime but condemned the "serious mismanagement" of his office. Following a closed-door hearing the following February, Glassboro borough officials announced that a settlement had been reached. Platt would retire, effective immediately — with his pension. The Times reported, "Platt, who received hugs and kisses from his supporters, some tearful, said he had no comment."

Two years later, after owning and operating the Broadway for nearly three decades, Platt opted to retire from movie theatre ownership as well. He had already sold off all of his other theatre assets, with the exception of the Glassboro Theatre (which would sit vacant until it was torn down in 2013). True to his word, he gave loyal Broadway staffer Dan Munyon first crack at buying the theatre from him. On May 13, 1999, along with business partner Charles Kern, Munyon's Family Theatre LLC purchased Pitman's Broadway Theatre from Platt Theatres Inc. for $225,000.

While the erstwhile owner of the Broadway remained a polarizing figure, Nathan Figlio, the son of Broadway organist Robert Figlio, gives credit where it's due. "My father once told me, 'People can say what they want about Duffy Platt, but at the time Platt owned the Broadway, old theatre organs were becoming very valuable. People were paying insane amounts of money for them.' My father said people were coming up to Platt weekly, asking, 'Can I buy the Broadway's Kimball?' and he refused to sell it. Even with all of his financial problems, Duffy Platt understood the value of keeping the Broadway's organ in the Broadway."

In exchange for close to a quarter of a million dollars (the amount it cost to build the Broadway in 1926), Dan Munyon had himself a disintegrating single-screen, second-run movie palace. And he couldn't have been happier. "Since I was 8 years old," he recalled, "I have always wanted to own a movie theatre." As the grandson of Mary Smith Munyon, a South Jersey vaudeville singer and dancer, Munyon was intent on returning live entertainment to the Broadway's stage. The theatre's new owner immediately set to work rebuilding the floors in the dressing rooms and green room. "The flooring was just gone," says Munyon. "You could bounce on it. I wanted to preserve the theatre and its legacy. And I wanted to keep it as close to the original as possible."

As only the third owner of the Broadway Theatre in its 73-year history, Munyon, 44, knew he was stepping into sizable shoes. "Mr. Wilkins opened the theatre as a silent movie house, successfully made the transition to sound and then ran the Broadway in the era when films were most popular," recounts Munyon. "When Mr. Platt came along, it was a different era. He excelled at doing live shows. He thrived in that."

As he set to work improving the theatre's interior, Munyon was also busy looking for the ideal inaugural live act to bring in under his new ownership. Dialing a talent agency, he told the rep on the other end he needed someone "as famous and as cheap as possible." The talent agent had the perfect fit — 79-year-old Hollywood legend Mickey Rooney and his wife, singer Jan Chamberlin, who had worked up "Two for the Show," a nationally touring cabaret act. Munyon immediately secured a February 26, 2000, booking at the Broadway. Explained Charles Kern: "Rooney is the perfect launch since he basically does a vaudeville-type act — comedy, singing and dancing — and the theatre has its roots in the art form."

Of their act, Rooney explained to the Gloucester County Times, "I come out and sing, my wife comes out and sings and then we both come out and sing." Of their rigorous touring schedule, Rooney explained, "We love to meet new people and rekindle old friendships." Added Chamberlin: "We're just people who love to entertain." During the interview, Rooney noted he was six

Poster for Mickey Rooney's February 26, 2000, appearance at the Broadway. Image courtesy of Daniel Munyon.

years older than the Pitman venue they were playing.

When Munyon received the couple's contract rider, he didn't blink at any of the requests. "I made sure they had everything on the list, down to picking out the red Skittles he didn't like," says Munyon. When Rooney arrived at the Broadway, his dressing room was precisely as he had requested and there was even a star on the door. Theorizes Munyon: "I think that's why he autographed so many things for us. He told me, 'I don't really sign things anymore, but you gave me everything on my list.' Getting to work with him backstage was a blast." Balcony seats for the appearance by the former MGM top box office attraction and Judy Garland's co-star went for $12; orchestra seats were $25. "Some people complained because he worked with a [tele]prompter," says Munyon. "But he was an older man in 2000. He sang, he told stories. She did Patsy Cline songs like Patsy Cline, but he was definitely the star. It was a great show. I just kept thinking, 'Mickey Rooney is on my stage.'" On his way out of Pitman, Rooney packed the star from his Broadway dressing room door.

In fall 2000, like Duffy Platt before him, Munyon had to go in front of the Pitman borough council when the churches again mobilized in response to his booking of "Dracula — A Ballet in Three Acts," set for Oct. 13-15. "I got reamed royally by the churches in town," remembers Munyon. "It felt a lot like when Mr. Platt got in trouble for the male dancers. They thought there was nudity in it." After Munyon assured the council the performance was rated PG-13 (in a ballet about a vampire, there were moments of blood and a couple of killings), he was allowed to proceed. Also on the agenda at the borough council — a business district revitalization project. The plan called for Broadway to be widened and water and sewer upgrades and other beautification projects implemented. By March 2001, there was a bulldozer parked in front of the theatre and No Parking signs were posted up and down Broadway. Adding to business owner frustrations, old sidewalks were dug up, making things a muddy mess when it rained. In its front-page story, the Times reported the road construction project could take anywhere from 90 to 120 days. As business on Broadway took a nosedive, Munyon, already financially stretched to the max and now deep in debt, wondered if he could make it through.

When road crews finally departed that summer and business returned to normal on Saturday nights, he breathed a sigh of relief. Munyon was delighted to give a Courier-Post reporter a tour of the theatre as he announced a new deal with a Philadelphia-based concert promoter to bring a series of live shows to the Broadway. The story ran on the front page of the Sunday, September 8, edition. But three days later, on the morning of Sept. 11, when terrorists hijacked four planes and crashed them into the World Trade Center, the Pentagon and a field in Pennsylvania, killing nearly 3,000, no one in America was thinking about going to the theatre.

Still, on September 27, 550 concertgoers, some wearing cowboy hats, were in the house for the Patty Loveless show at the Broadway. It was the biggest crowd Munyon had generated under his ownership. Like Duffy Platt in 1977 when Donna Fargo had packed the house, Munyon was ecstatic. "There's no better place to see a band than an old theatre," attested attendee Lee Whitaker of Haddon Heights. "It has a special ambiance."

In December, with the theatre's iconic Kimball organ now fully restored thanks to the Southern Jersey chapter of the American Theatre Organ Society, Munyon decided to celebrate the instrument's resurrection with a special screening of "A Dog's Life," Charlie Chaplin's 1918 silent classic. With help from the SJ-ATOS, Munyon was able to book famed theatre organist Dennis James, the in-house player at Hollywood's El Capitan Theatre, to provide the live accompaniment. "With the Kimball restored, we wanted to re-create that era for people," Munyon recalls. More than 500 classic-film fans showed up for the screening and live concert. Reflecting on his group's eight-year odyssey to revive the 75-year-old instrument (an estimated $175,000 in donated labor and parts), SJ-ATOS member Joe Rementer, then 64, reflected, "In my youth, I never realized what was in them. They have a very happy sound."

Someone who had more than a passing acquaintance with the Broadway Kimball's "happy sound" had just moved back to New Jersey from Colorado and was auditioning for the open organist position at the theatre — Nathan Figlio, the son of former Broadway organist Robert Figlio. Like his dad 30 years earlier, Figlio got the gig. Having grown up in a house with a pipe organ and spending his childhood at the Broadway, Nathan was a perfect fit for the position. "Unlike church organs, theatre organs were designed to be a one-person orchestra, complete with drums, bells, sound effects, etc.," explains Figlio. "The theatre organist is the conductor, musicians, arranger and orchestrator all in one. The Broadway's Kimball has three keyboards that add a bit more complexity to things as well. It helps to be highly coordinated. Playing it is a full-body exercise."

Second-generation Broadway organist Nathan Figlio.

By January 2002, Munyon's roller coaster ride of Broadway ownership plunged again on a downward trajectory when Conectiv Electric disconnected the theatre after Munyon's $13,500 bill remained unpaid. Citing the paralyzing road improvement project and 9/11, Munyon told the Courier-Post, "It sent me on a downward spiral I have not been able to recover from yet. I'm still digging myself out of this mess." The Broadway remained dark for a week in the town's already-precarious business district filled with vacancies. Finally, on Jan. 25, thanks to "a bunch of friends who pitched in and gave me enough money to cover it," the lights were back on inside the Broadway in time for Munyon to run a weekend double feature of Pixar's "Monsters, Inc." and the comedy "Not Another Teen Movie."

Up and down Broadway, the economic realities of the early 2000s were taking their toll on local businesses as shops continued to close. Dan Munyon, wife Mary Ann and their five children became the Broadway's key staff. By July 2003, the bank demanded full payment on Munyon's loan and back mortgage payments totaling $253,000. Just two hours before the Gloucester County sheriff was set to auction off the historic structure, Munyon short-circuited the sale by filing for Chapter 11 bankruptcy. "I've hit rock bottom," Munyon told The Philadelphia Inquirer as patrons trickled in for a matinee screening of "The Hulk." "Everything I have is here. I will have wasted so many years if I lose it now." The paper also reached out to historian Allen Hauss, who was researching his 2006 book "South Jersey Movie Houses." "The Broadway is the last real jewel left," said Hauss. "There's nothing as intricate or as unique as that theatre anywhere near Philadelphia. If it closes, it will be a devastating loss for this region's history." Shop owners on Broadway were also worried about the street's anchor attraction shuttering. "That theatre's been the focal point in this town since 1926," said Joan Fox of the Snooty Fox collectibles shop. "And it's important it stays that way."

Broadway Theatre supporters, including Louis Centanni, a 17-year-old local actor, banded together to sponsor fundraisers. Centanni, who grew up in Pitman, saw his first film, "Free Willy," inside the historic movie palace. "The Broadway played a big part in why I'm an actor," he told the Courier-Post. "I want the theatre to survive not just because it's part of my history but because it's part of the community's history."

On the evening of Dec. 1, 2003, the Broadway Theatre's financial troubles paled in comparison to what was happening down the street. Just before 7 p.m., a Broadway resident living in the apartment across the way looked out her window and saw smoke billowing from the attic of the 108-year-old Pitman United Methodist Church. Within minutes, flames were consuming the roof of the structure as fire departments from across South Jersey responded to the six-alarm blaze. Down at the Broadway, Dan Munyon was about to roll the 7 p.m. movie when police showed up, shouting, "You've got to get out!" Guiding patrons outside, Munyon saw embers flying across the street in the theatre's direction. His son Matthew rushed to hook up a garden hose and began dousing the theatre's roof. By 10 p.m., the fire was under control, but a large section of the church's roof was gone. Hundreds of people, many crying, hugging each other and wrapped in blankets, watched as the hook and ladders knocked down the remaining flames. "The church is a total loss," said Pitman Mayor Bruce Ware. The Pitman Methodist Church was not only a landmark for its 900 members but a symbol that predated the town's founding, going back to 1871, when summer camp meetings were first held in the Pitman Grove.

Thankfully, no one was injured in the fire. "The church is the heart of the community," said Mayor Ware. He looked around at his fellow Pitmanites shivering in the street and added, "We are stumbling right now and the community will help. That's what Pitman is — everyone helps out." A reporter on the scene spotted the church's Rev. Lanie Price, clustered with members of her congregation across the street. He approached and asked, "How do you feel now that your church is gone?" An emotional Price paused for a moment and replied, "The church is not burning down; a church building is burning down. The church is standing here with me. The church is not a building, but its people."

Forty-eight hours later, contractors worked to remove the PUMC's steeple so traffic could be reopened on Broadway. Church organist Susan Lanning Crispin had convinced Rev. Price to let her don a hard hat and enter the structure. Minutes later, she emerged from the burned structure to cheers. Crispin held aloft — miraculously unscathed — the church's mission statement sign. It had been painted by her father William O. Lanning, the church's longtime financial secretary. The sign had hung outside the church sanctuary for 25 years. In turn, Bill Lanning was carrying on a family tradition dating back decades. His father, William L. Lanning, had painted the iconic "Everybody Likes Pitman" sign next to the city limits back in 1913.

The Pitman United Methodist mission statement read: "Our Purpose: That every person know Jesus Christ as Savior and Lord, That we create a climate where spiritual growth occurs, So that God's will to save the lost is accomplished. Glory to God."

The following Sunday, Dec. 7, 2003, was a busy day at the Broadway. There was an afternoon Pitman Hobo Band concert, a screening of the 1965 John Wayne-Kirk Douglas war picture "In Harm's Way" and an evening showing of the new Hugh Grant-led ensemble romantic comedy "Love, Actually." And thanks to an invitation from Dan Munyon, the displaced members of Pitman United Methodist Church prayed together during Sunday morning services held at the theatre.

In return, the beleaguered owner of the Broadway was about to experience a much-needed blessing from the Almighty himself.

Broadway ad. Courtesy of Daniel Munyon.

Broadway owner Dan Munyon with wife Mary Ann (L) receiving a proclamation in 2004 from Gloucester County Freeholders. Photo courtesy of Daniel Munyon.

CHAPTER NINE

"I feel like I failed the community."
2004–2006

It was an ideal movie to book in a town founded as a Methodist summer camp. But Dan Munyon, navigating a steep climb out of bankruptcy, lacked the financing to spring for any first-run movie, let alone a biblical epic directed by Mel Gibson. But because "The Passion of the Christ" was independently distributed, Munyon reached out to the film's local distributor, Galaxy Theatres and posed a single question: "Do you need another screen?"

When the voice on the other end of the phone asked, "How many you got?" Munyon replied, "One, but it will be dedicated completely to your film." An agreement was struck. Munyon could run "Passion" at the Broadway — if he could come up with a $5,000 deposit. The theatre owner went to his family for feedback and they urged him to proceed. After all, churches across South Jersey were gassing up their vans and scheduling field trips to see the R-rated film starring Jim Caviezel depicting the final — and violently bloody — 12 hours of Christ's life. Munyon crunched the numbers and realized that if he could sell enough advance church-group tickets, he could raise the $5K deposit he needed.

"The word 'crucifixion' has become neutered," explained Washington Township evangelist Dan Cooper to the Gloucester County Times on why he was organizing an outing for his flock. "A better word is execution. Jesus was executed for us. There are no other Christian faith-based movies that have the potential impact that this one does."

Thanks to advance ticket sales, Munyon came up with the $5,000 deposit. And for the first time in the four years since purchasing the Broadway, he had a first-run film on the screen. Appropriately, "The Passion of the Christ" opened in Pitman on Ash Wednesday.

Christians flooded in the front doors to see the biblical drama. The Broadway's phone, to which service had just been restored, began ringing nonstop. "As soon as the film got on the screen, churches started calling me up," recounts Munyon. "They wanted to buy hundreds of tickets at a time." A front-page story in the Times, "'Passion' May Be Savior for Pitman Theatre," helped sales as well. "Everyday I'm struggling with what can shut me down," Munyon told the paper. "This could financially help me out a lot. It will bring people into our town. We're not going under. I have a first-run film. I'm still running."

The Broadway Theatre's single-screen first-week box office gross for the film was $17,983. Week two generated $7,261. "The Passion of the Christ" ended up enjoying a six-week run at the Broadway. "When you get that many people in the door," Munyon explains, "I was making enough in concession sales alone to pay the mortgage."

Now that he could show first-run films again, Munyon hoped to maintain the momentum "Passion" had sparked at the Broadway.

In May, with supporter and local actor Louis Centanni dressed as a 1940s movie usher and Gloucester County Senior Services' Lorraine Beckett looking on, Dan Munyon was back in the Times – this time to promote his new Wednesday-afternoon senior matinees at the Broadway, featuring classic films like "The Philadelphia Story" and "Casablanca." Organist Harold Ware provided a 30-minute concert on the Kimball before each screening.

Later in the month, with emcee Centanni dressed as the Cowardly Lion, Munyon booked two of the surviving Munchkins from the 1939 classic for a weekend of "Sing-Along With the Wizard of Oz" screenings. Jerry Maren, 84,

Dan Munyon and actor Louis Centanni, with Jerry Maren and Karl Slover from the cast of 1939's "The Wizard of Oz." Photo courtesy of Daniel Munyon.

who had uttered the phrase "We represent the Lollipop Guild" in the film and Karl Slover, 86, who played four roles, came in for the event. After each screening, the pair did a 30-minute Q&A and then signed autographs. Outside, a yellow brick road greeted patrons near the box office. Maren and Slover recalled they got paid $300 for six weeks of work on the picture. "In the 1930s, $50 a week was considered good pay," remembered Slover. "Especially since the 124 little people on the set were essentially extras." Added Maren: "I still just want to get up from my easy chair and dance to my 'Lollipop Guild' [song] each time it comes on screen." Over 60 years later, Slover still had the "Oz" cast salary memorized. Jack Haley as the Tin Man scored $3,000 a week, he recalled, while Bert Lahr as the Cowardly Lion fetched $2,500. Garland pulled down $500 and Toto wrangled $125, compared with his $50. "I guess Toto had a better agent," shrugged Slover.

For Christmas 2004, Munyon found a 35mm copy of the Frank Capra classic "It's a Wonderful Life," which hadn't been screened at the theatre since its original lackluster 1947 release. "I had the advantage of time," Munyon explains with a laugh. "Whatever it was in 1947 that caused people not to see it was a thing of the past. By 2004, thanks to all of the airings on TV, it became a Christmas tradition. People really loved seeing it on the big screen." For Munyon, it was easy to see why the film resonated with locals: "When you look at the Bedford Falls streetscape, the buildings and that time period, it's Pitman."

A year later, Munyon and wife Mary Ann debuted the Vaudeville Café in the Broadway's second-floor lobby in hopes of selling desserts and coffee between movies. They secured furniture for the new café by repurposing items thrown away when the business next door closed. "The idea," Munyon told the Times, "is that people enjoy being in a place that is elegant and might want something more than popcorn."

The Broadway also received a boost when the Camden Courier-Post ran a feature on South Jersey theatre revivals. The now-retired Duffy Platt was in a reflective mood as he discussed his history at the Broadway. "I remember vaudeville and acts like Edgar Bergen and Charlie McCarthy playing there in 1939. I was a kid back then. Those were good times. It was a good place to go. It's part of the heritage of the town." Dan Munyon told the paper he hoped to emerge from bankruptcy the following month.

Instead, following a screening of "Robots" on March 29, 2005, the Broadway went dark after a bankruptcy court judge placed the theatre under the control of a court-appointed trustee. Munyon owed more than $270,000 on his existing mortgage. U.S. Bankruptcy Judge Judith Wizmur also converted Munyon's bankruptcy case from Chapter 11 to Chapter 7 liquidation. While the courts decided the fate of the theatre, members of the still-displaced Pitman United Methodist Church were allowed to gather for Sunday worship at the shuttered venue. Church organist Sue Lanning Crispin, who had first performed on the instrument in 1975 as Miss Pitman, now played hymns on the theatre's Kimball for Easter services.

In April, Judge Wizmur ordered that trustees had 90 days to sell the Broadway. Among the interested buyers: the Lenape Regional Performing Arts Center. "The intention has always been to keep the building a theatre," Russell Johnson, president of the Greater Pitman Chamber of Commerce, told the Times. "Having it as a theatre brings the most vitality and foot traffic to the downtown." A Courier-Post editorial, "Pitman's Broadway Theatre Worth Saving," argued, "Just because it can no longer compete with the first-run multiplexes doesn't mean the theatre should join the list of empty properties on Broadway. A return to its roots as a venue for live shows could very well be what saves this theatre."

The Broadway's familiar red-lettered marquee now read: "Save the Broadway," with a phone number that rang across the street in the Snooty Fox, the gift shop owned by Joan Fox, who was helping to raise money for the historic structure.

In the summer of 2005, the Borough of Pitman celebrated its centennial by debuting a brand-new slogan: "The Small Town With a Big Heart." But unlike its weeklong festivities in 1955, the Broadway was not part of the town's 100th birthday. The theatre remained shuttered. In their feature documentary "Pitman: A Centennial Celebration," released on DVD to mark the occasion, writer-narrators Bruce Lowden and Ralph Richards Jr. described the venue, saying, "Although having a bit of a struggle today, the Broadway has a reputation of a grand old theatre."

For Pitman residents and Dan Munyon, the next year felt like a ride on the old Alcyon Park toboggan roller coaster — full of unexpected twists and turns. In July, Judge Wizmur approved the sale of the theatre to a Camden County talent agent for $450,000, but the deal fell through when the buyer couldn't come up with the full financing. At one point, a $520,000 bid by a Haddonfield teenager was briefly considered. By the fall, with help from $14,309 in donations from about 200 Pitman residents, Judge Wizmur agreed to let Munyon buy back the Broadway — for $490,000. But the deal disintegrated when financing through a mortgage broker couldn't be finalized.

On October 24, 2005, Dan Munyon took time out from his financial troubles to mourn the passing of his former boss. Clayton "Duffy" Platt, the man who had sold him his dream business in 1999, was dead. The controversial former Broadway Theatre owner and grandson of Pitman Mayor Andrew Trucksess was 74. "Duffy loved the theatre and formerly owned and operated both the Glassboro Theatre and Broadway Theatre," his death notice stated. "He also enjoyed the Jersey shore, boating, fishing and the outdoors. He is predeceased by his mother Mildred and sister Mimi. He leaves behind a large circle of friends who have known him for many years and will miss him terribly."

The Broadway remained shuttered throughout the 2005 holiday season for the first time in its 79-year history, as the Gloucester County Sheriff's Department scheduled and then postponed its sale multiple times. "It's between lawyers right now," Munyon told the Times. He was busy in talks with investors attempting to finance a new loan. Pitman native Mike Doughty recalls that era on Broadway well. "As the theatre declined, so did the town. You would drive down Broadway and see all of these closed-up storefronts. There was no reason to walk uptown unless your newspaper got wet and you needed to go up to Pownall's News Agency to swap it out."

Pitman native Peter Slack was among those troubled by the shuttered theatre on his daily three-mile jog that began behind the theatre and ended in front of its weathered marquee. Like countless other Pitman kids, Slack fondly recalled lobbing jujubes at the screen while attending Saturday matinees to see Disney fare like "Old Yeller" for a quarter. He once snuck into a vacant box seat to watch "The Sword in the Stone." He kissed his first date there. By 2006, Slack was running his family's 100-year-old business, Slack Medical Publishing Inc., a national company based in West Deptford. Jogging past the Broadway, Slack began to think "what if?"

Darrell Blood in a still from filmmaker Jason Weber's short YouTube documentary on the Broadway's renovation.

Former borough solicitor Warren Carr had been among the folks encouraging Slack to become the fourth owner of the town's best-known historic building. "At the time, I was acting on behalf of the town planning board," recalls Carr. "I prodded Peter, telling him, 'You ought to buy this.'" Even his assistant, DonaLee Shirley Milner, who had grown up on Ardmore Avenue behind the Little League field where Slack had played as a kid, was employing a squeeze play on her boss in hopes he would purchase the theatre. His curiosity piqued, Slack called the bank that held the note and asked if he could tour the theatre. He asked his vice president of finance, Darrell Blood, to meet him at the Broadway.

"I knew absolutely nothing about the theatre," remembers Blood. He actually drove past the 1926 structure, nestled among other closed businesses, on the way to meet Slack. "I thought it was going to be this little 100-seat theatre," Blood remembers. "And then we walked into this big thousand-seat place that was completely hidden from the street."

"The theatre was not in good shape at all," recalls Slack. When Blood placed his hand on one of the theatre auditorium's walls, it crumbled beneath his touch. "I was ready to walk out the door, but Darrell kept looking around." Explains Blood: "I saw an opportunity there. These kinds of places just don't exist anymore. But where I saw opportunity, Peter saw mold, mildew and things falling down. It was basically ready to be torn down." Remembers Slack: "We both shook our heads and I said, 'Whoever gets this has a *real* big job ahead of them.'"

Finally, on February 1, 2006, at the Gloucester County Justice Complex in Woodbury, after months of anxious anticipation, Pitman's Broadway Theatre was officially put up for sheriff's sale. Among those in attendance: former owner Dan Munyon, his attorney William Macklin and Pitman Chamber of Commerce President Russ Johnson. Veronica Goodman, a local talent agent who had tried to save the historic Harwan Theatre in Mount Ephraim from the wrecking ball, was also there. And thanks to a phone call from Darrell Blood asking his boss, "Hey, wanna go over to the sheriff's sale?," Peter Slack was present. While it had cost a quarter to get into the Saturday matinee when Slack was a boy, on Groundhog Day Eve 2006, the Broadway's price of admission was quite a bit steeper.

Slack, Blood and Johnson sat in the back of the judge's chambers and watched. Just in case, Darrell Blood had brought along a cashier's check made out for $100,000. ("Keep that check firmly in your pocket," advised Slack.) On the other end of Russ Johnson's cellphone was Pitman councilman Michael D. Batten Jr., who was listening in on the proceedings. The opening bid was $10,000. Eventually, Slack stood and placed a bid of $303,000. But then Veronica Goodman offered $307,000. "My stomach was churning," recalls Batten. "As a member of the council, I didn't want to be one of the people who would have to make a decision to tear down 80 years of the town's history. None of us did."

Dejected, seeing Goodman buy his former theatre, Munyon departed the sale. Of his client's unsuccessful last-ditch effort to buy back the Broadway, Munyon's attorney Macklin explained to the Courier-Post: "Dan was given assurances he would have financing without contingencies. Those promises were not kept."

The drive home was a long one for Dan Munyon. "I feel like I failed the community," he reflects. "I still do all these years later. I would walk down the street and kids would call me the 'Movie Man.' I was proud of giving kids a safe place to come and enjoy themselves. As I tell my wife, I'm not the brightest star in the sky. I don't like failure. I'm not personally afraid of failing, but I was afraid of failing my family and failing to keep the Broadway building alive."

Back at the Justice Complex in Woodbury, clerks were attempting to collect payment from Veronica Goodman. "There was some kind of chaos going on up in the front of the room," Russ Johnson remembers. "Like a jigsaw puzzle, [Goodman] was trying to piece together this flurry of checks to put down the necessary 20 percent payment." As Slack got up to leave, Johnson put out his arm and asked him to wait a second.

"When she went to pay the sheriff, she had these checks that she tried to endorse over," recalls Slack. The sheriff would only accept a certified check. Goodman's bid was then declined. The Broadway Theatre went back on the block. When no other bidders materialized, Slack's bid of $303,000 was reconsidered. Darrell Blood then pulled from his pocket the cashier's check he had proactively prepared and handed it to his boss.

And so on the eve of the silent movie house's 80th birthday, Slack, 49, became the Broadway's new owner. Grinning, Pitman Chamber President Russ Johnson told a reporter, "We got everything we wanted today." Before exiting, Slack fielded a final question from Courier-Post reporter Tim Zatzariny Jr.: What did he know about running a movie theatre? Smiling, the Pitman theatre's fourth owner replied, "Nothing, but I've got good advisors."

That night, Slack, wife Jill and their children toured their crumbling new acquisition. Recalls Slack: "We were shaking our heads and asking ourselves, What are we going to do? Movies? Live performances? What do we do with the thing?" Reflecting on the family's purchase nearly 20 years later, Jill Slack answers the obvious question with a laugh. "Did it upend my life? Sure it did. But it was important to us because we lived here and we were raising our children here. Pitman was turning into a complete ghost town. There was nothing here but a pizzeria." Staring at the partially collapsed balcony, Peter Slack was certain of one thing: "The theatre needed to reopen as soon as possible. The town was suffering."

Three days after the purchase, a Courier-Post editorial concurred with Slack's assessment. "Having the highly visible theatre sit dark hasn't seemed right since it closed 11 months ago. The Broadway has history, charm and a special place in the hearts of many Pitman residents. Whether it's movies or live shows, hopefully area residents will again embrace the theatre and return. Without patrons, Slack or any other owner can't make a theatre a success."

Remembers Pitman native Michael L. Razze Jr.: "It was a bleak time. We were losing stores downtown we had been accustomed to seeing forever. There were all of these rumors like there was a Haddonfield family who wanted to buy the theatre and turn it into an indoor skate park. And then Peter and Jill stepped in and there was this immediate sense of relief. We all knew Peter and Jill."

"I did this to help my town come back," Slack explained to The Philadelphia Inquirer. "This is a unique place where kids still walk to school. The downtown has declined the last 10 years, but I think it has tremendous potential. It is just a couple of steps from turning a corner."

But taking those couple of steps wasn't going to be cheap. For starters, just after Slack bought the Broadway, Darrell Blood fielded an inquiry from the bank — would

Slack like to purchase the theatre's interior assets? Blood recalls, "I'm like, '*What*?!' I was told, 'What you bought was the building.' The fixtures, including the seats, were separate." The bank, Blood and Slack then negotiated an additional $15,000 for everything inside.

"There's a lot of work that needs to be done," was Patricia Mangano's assessment to the Gloucester County Times. Mangano, former production manager for the Ritz Theatre in Haddon Township, had been hired to spearhead the Broadway's reopening efforts. The theatre's marquee was now helping to spread the word: "Clean Up Volunteers Needed," with a phone number. In addition to a flurry of phone calls, Mangano had to contend with unexpected guests inviting themselves inside. "I found two people standing on the stage the other day," she told the Courier-Post. "They were the cutest elderly couple, reminiscing about the theatre. The gentleman showed me a 1982 ticket from the time he came here to see Johnny Cash."

At 8 a.m. on Saturday, April 29, 2006, the Broadway's 80-year-old doors opened to the public once again — for a community cleanup. More than 100 Pitmanites, many of whom had gone to their first movies as kids at the Broadway, reported for duty. Onstage, a grateful Peter Slack, dressed in jeans, work shirt and white cap, told the assembled, "I want to thank everyone for coming out. This is the largest crowd we've had in this theatre in a long, long time." The volunteers applauded. Nearly 20 years later, Slack recalls, "People just showed up on a Saturday morning and said, 'Here I am, I've got my work boots and my gloves. What can I do?' It meant a lot. Everybody in Pitman grew up in the theatre. They had fond memories and wanted to help bring the theatre back."

Among those volunteers was Pitman native James C. Brown, who showed up with his camcorder to shoot footage of the decaying venue. Having watched Hammer horror films like "Taste the Blood of Dracula" as a kid at the Broadway, Brown had a lifelong connection to the theatre. "It was exciting to see behind the scenes," says Brown. Less exciting were Brown's duties for the day. Dumpsters lined Theatre Avenue and volunteers quickly got to work, filling them with trash, old carpeting and wallpaper and even a long-expired Christmas tree.

Community cleanup day at the Broadway, April 29, 2006. Screenshot from Jason Weber's short YouTube documentary.

Russ Johnson, Pitman Chamber of Commerce president and a brand-new member of the theatre's advisory board, meanwhile, was assigned to the balcony. "My job was ripping out the old carpeting," says Johnson. "I think I blew black soot out of my nose for a month after that cleanup. But what I remember most were the people sharing stories — their first dates as teenagers, being in the Miss Pitman pageant on the stage. Everyone had a connection."

To oversee the renovation efforts, Slack had assembled a dream team of Pitmanites — Walter Madison, Pitman councilman and owner of Madison Painting; Baldwin Home Improvement owner Kenny Baldwin, a Pitman general contractor who had ushered at the Broadway as a teenager; and longtime resident and community volunteer Watson "Watty" Lohmann.

Other volunteers wearing protective masks began scraping decades of chewing gum off the floor and the bottoms of chairs. Workers cleaning out the clutter from the general manager's office discovered an old signed Tammy Wynette concert contract from the 1970s. As Pitman High graduate and filmmaker Jason Weber shot footage for a planned documentary on the Broadway's rebirth, Baldwin, perched on a ladder, relayed, "This is just the dirty work. Now the hard work starts." Pat Mangano was impressed by the turnout and the town's dedication to the cleanup effort. Restoration organizers ended up with a volunteer list filled with the names of 150 Pitmanites eager to come back to help. Said Mangano: "Not only did we have 100 people come out the day of the cleanup, they didn't go away."

With one exception.

Walt Madison's brand-new painting assistant took one look at the peeling walls, leaking roof and collapsed balcony and promptly tendered his resignation. As a hole was cut in the wall in an attempt to inspect the stability of the auditorium's original plaster, sparks started flying. Madison quickly discovered the original 1926 walls had been constructed of wire-mesh plaster, which made attempting to repair it 80 years later virtually impossible. It would all have to come out. "After everyone else had left the cleanup day, I was there by myself," Madison recalls. "The theatre doors were open and the light was streaming in. I just remember sitting there staring at the crumbling theatre and thinking, 'What the hell have I gotten myself into?'"

In his comments to the Courier-Post, Pitman chamber president Russ Johnson could have been channeling William Lacy and Abe Applebaum, the two men who in 1925 were determined to raze the old Carr mansion to create an economic engine for Pitman. "The theatre is the focal point of downtown," said Johnson. "Theatres lead to restaurants and restaurants lead to evening culture and evening culture will benefit our merchants." The May 21 article previewed Peter Slack's intended time frame for re-opening — tickets to a September black-tie-optional fundraising gala would go on sale in mid-June. The venue's new business name, as registered with the state Department of Treasury and the U.S. Patent and Trademark Office, was The Broadway Theatre of Pitman.

While structural engineers inspecting the Broadway assured Peter Slack the 80-year-old building had "good bones," a restoration architect offered a dire assessment of the interior structure. The leaks in the roof had resulted in water getting into the theatre's walls. "They told us, 'These walls need to be sealed up immediately and you need to get air conditioning flowing ASAP,'" recalled Slack. "Otherwise, we were this close to losing the building. He even gave us a time frame of six to eight weeks before all of the money we were spending would be for naught."

Walls were replaced and sealed up and HVAC repairs commenced immediately. Finding the leaks in the theatre's flat roof, however, was a trial-and-error process. "A leak could be coming in a corner of the theatre, but its origin might be 100 yards away on the roof," explains Walt Madison. "I had a roofer on speed dial for months." Finally, the last leak was located and the balcony was rebuilt.

Then there were the electrical concerns. An electrical company was hired to address the building's aging wiring. Ten master electricians were dispatched to work on the massive project for six weeks. At the end, they presented Darrell Blood with a bill for $250,000. Later, Blood discovered that the electricians had used an outdated electrical code and the entire building would have to be redone to bring the Broadway up to current codes. Lawyers got involved. "After all this," reasons Slack, "we definitely did not want a fire."

Meanwhile, Walt Madison was busy up on a 40-foot ladder painting most of the theatre himself. "There were about 2 feet of pink in the proscenium [the arch of the stage] that we couldn't reach," recalls Madison. "The organ was in the way." Unlike other historic theatres that employ teams of archivists and keep decades of paint chips and fabric swatch records on hand, Madison had to work without historical documentation.

"I did it one color at a time," he says. "Sherwin-Williams is less than a block away. I would eyeball the color we needed and then go over and get a quart of paint. I'd try it on the wall, bring it back and say, 'That's not it. Put some more white or some more red in it.' I went back and forth until I got it right. It was completely trial and error. We tried to keep everything as close as humanly possible to what had been on the wall." Other tasks were easier for the painting team. "All the gold trim in there?" says Madison. "That's all Krylon gold spray paint. We must have gone through 20 cases to redo all of the gold in the theatre." There were mishaps along the way. One day, working on a 20-foot ladder on the landing in the lobby, Madison placed it at too sharp an angle and fell. "You're supposed to tuck and roll," he remembers. "I didn't do either. It was more like a splat." At the ER, Madison learned he had broken off the end of his elbow. Pins had to be inserted during surgery. "Luckily," says Madison, "the paint roller fit in my sling." When it was time to tackle the theatre's massive ceiling, despite some initial protestations, Madison was talked into using scaffolding guardrails.

Meanwhile, the Broadway's iconic crystal chandeliers had to be lowered via a hand crank and cleaned ("It takes about 20 minutes per chandelier," Madison recalls). While some affected walls could be rebuilt, there was no way to save the old plaster in the stairways leading to the theatre's box seats. But beneath the plaster, Walt Madison discovered the theatre's original brick walls. "We ended up leaving the brick exposed," he remembers. "It's now one of my favorite things about the theatre. I felt reassured when I later visited the Ben Franklin House in Philadelphia and learned they had done the same thing."

One of the Broadway's original artifacts Madison hated most to part with was the massive asbestos fire curtain adorned with a Japanese garden painting. "It was gorgeous, but we had to get rid of it," he reflects. "We had to cut it down. It took two of us." Ten new fire doors were installed. The original 1,200-seat venue lost some of its seating due to handicapped seating regulations and the construction of a new state-of-the-art production booth. When the addition of a handicapped-accessible bathroom was projected to cost $25,000, Pitman councilman Gene Shoemaker (the son of former Pitman Mayor Robert Shoemaker) worked with Kenny Baldwin and a plumber to do the work for $3,000.

Michael Razze Jr. and wife Tammy DeLucas Razze, who had once competed on the Broadway stage in the Miss Pitman pageant, were among those returning to volunteer at the theatre where they had spent their childhoods. Tammy was in the balcony, assigned to clean the theatre's original 1926 wooden seats. "I don't even want to think about how long some of the gum had been there," she says, laughing. "But overall, the balcony chairs were in good shape." Downstairs, Michael was busy polishing the brass rails around the boxes from which he'd once watched his then-girlfriend walk the Miss Pitman runway. "Whenever you would finish a task, you'd go to Walt, Kenny or Watty and they'd send you off to do something else," recalls Razze. To fulfill their bronze service award, the members of Pitman Girl Scout Troop 66536 spent weeks polishing all of the brass surfaces in the Broadway.

For months, the volunteer repair and restoration project continued as the Kimball organ received a tuneup, seats were cleaned and reupholstered, new carpeting was laid, fresh paint was applied to new drywall, wallpaper was installed and old film projectors were repaired. Most importantly, the Broadway's 70-year-old iconic neon peacock marquee was carefully cleaned, repaired and repainted as workers dangled from the top of a 12-foot ladder. ("That's a short ladder for me," says Madison, who was once hired to repaint the letters on the side of the Washington Township water tower.)

For 12 days, Walt Madison and volunteer Nick Cattafi power-washed and scraped the bottom of the marquee, de-rusted and repainted, rewired sockets and reinstalled the sign's 100 light bulbs. "I had to match the original colors as closely as possible," recalls Madison. "If you look closely, it's actually five different colors up there and you had to get that light green color that distinguishes the marquee exactly right. Otherwise, I'd have never heard the end of it from everyone in town." The sign's transformers, a victim of the elements, had to be replaced and waterproofed as well. Finally, all the glass neon on the sign had to be reblown and reinstalled.

On Friday, Aug. 11, 2006, at 7 p.m., Broadway was closed off when Pitmanites gathered with baby strollers, children and pets to celebrate the theatre's rebirth with a ceremonial relighting of the marquee. Pitman's Hobo Band was on hand to perform. "I think it shows a lot of faith on the part of Peter Slack to invest in this community and faith in the community to invest in the theatre," said Mayor Alice Polocz, who was the proprietor of Bob's Hobbies and Crafts a few doors down from the theatre. "There have been studies that say, 'The way downtown goes, the way the town goes.' I am hoping the theatre will draw other businesses into town." Added Slack: "This is our way of celebrating that we are close to reopening our doors, as well as recognizing all of the hard work that's been done by volunteers from Pitman and our neighboring communities."

At dusk, hundreds of attendees, many holding red and white balloons emblazoned with the theatre's logo, ap-

Pitman councilman and renovation painter Walt Madison, dancing in front of the refurbished marquee, August 2006. Photo courtesy of Peter Slack.

plauded when Mayor Polocz hit the switch and the rainbow neon peacock marquee blazed to life again for the first time in 17 months. Leaving nothing to chance, Walt Madison had tested the marquee repeatedly before the public unveiling.

One of those cheering from his lawn chair was Bill Lanning, 87, who had attended the Broadway's public debut back in 1926. "This was the spot of Pitman; it really brought the town to life," Lanning recalled to the Times. Pointing to the crowd around him, he added, "You see how it draws the people, so it must mean something to them." But it was Broadway restoration painter and councilman Walt Madison who perhaps best captured the emotion of the moment: "I think the glow all over South Jersey tonight is coming from Pitman. There's a full moon, but it's Pitman that's lighting up the sky."

The wording on the Broadway's marquee was now changed to "Subscribe Now," a nod to Patricia Mangano and Darrell Blood's planned pivot for the venue. Weeks earlier, Mangano, a veteran of the Ritz Theatre in Haddon Township, had asked if she could attend a meeting of the theatre's new board of directors at Slack's residence. There she pitched the idea of a subscriber-based annual Broadway musical mainstage season. Slack recalls, "I remember thinking, 'My God, that's the best idea we've heard!' Subscriptions would give us the working capital to keep the theatre up and running." Adds Blood: "It made perfect sense since Pat knew the theatre people and knew the shows." Beginning in January 2007, in addition to running films, the Broadway would produce a live theatre season.

With the closest competing Broadway musical mainstage across the bridge at the Walnut Street Theatre in Philadelphia, Mangano and Blood's ambitious idea was to book, audition and stage six shows each year under the leadership of producing artistic director Charles C. Gill. In filmmaker Jason Weber's documentary on the Broadway's restoration, Gill predicted, "The town will embrace us, but they will also expect good solid entertainment and I think we can give them that. I *know* we can give them that." To entice new subscribers, Blood had set a season rate at just $65 for all six of the 2007 mainstage productions.

When Peter Slack asked Blood how the theatre could possibly make money with such a business plan, Blood's reply could have been cribbed from Clayton Platt's 1977 country music profitability playbook. "Volume," explains Blood. "I call it stupid pricing. Who wouldn't pay that for six shows? I told Peter, 'If you do it cheap enough, people will come.'" A skeptical Slack suggested a side bet with Blood about how many Broadway subscribers would sign up for the planned 2007 theatrical season. Blood promptly took the bet.

Slack was true to his word and with his work crew of Walt Madison, Kenny Baldwin and Watty Lohmann – plus

150 Pitmanites volunteering around the clock – the theatre restoration was completed in record time. On Sept. 23, 2006, a black-tie-optional "Bring Back Broadway" Gala at the theatre would be hosted by the Greater Pitman Chamber of Commerce and Heritage of Pitman Inc. Overwhelmed by the amount of work at the start of the restoration, Walt Madison finally allowed himself to celebrate the theatre's rebirth on the morning of the gala. "I had gone out to rent a floor buffer so I could polish the lobby," recalls Madison. "When we got done buffing the floor, polishing the last piece of brass and touching up the last bit of paint, it finally began to feel real to me. We literally went from our paint clothes to changing into our tuxes."

While he had paid $303,000 for the Broadway back in February, Peter Slack had then invested another million into getting the refurbished, renovated and restored theatre ready for its grand reopening.

Just one thing stood in the path of getting the town's iconic economic engine back firing on all cylinders. Specifically, this obstacle was on the other end of a disbelieving Darrell Blood's phone. It was the Pitman fire marshal, who was refusing to sign the Broadway's new certificate of occupancy.

Owner Peter Slack welcomes guests to the reopening of the Broadway Theatre, September 23, 2006. Photo courtesy of the Slack family.

CHAPTER TEN

"Peter Slack could have done anything with his money, but he chose to help the town."

2006–2016

The blazing spotlights – courtesy of the Pitman Fire Company No. 1 generator truck – once again illuminated the Broadway Theatre. Under the freshly painted neon peacock marquee, hundreds of formally attired gala attendees strolled the velvet-rope-lined red carpet to enter the fully renovated theatre. Pitman's own opera star Barbara Dever had returned home to perform for the Sept. 23, 2006, fundraiser, as did Miss New Jersey 2004 and Miss Pitman 1999 Erica-Lynne Scanlon. Veteran Gloucester County Times columnist Bob Shryock made sure he was on the guest list.

"I'm terminally old school and stubbornly resist changes," Shryock conceded to readers. "That's why I'm euphoric about the reopening of the Broadway Theatre. It's changed, yes, but in the right way. Through the vision and commitment of the Slack family and through one of the county's most extraordinary mass volunteer efforts ever, the grand old lady has been refurbished magnificently."

The columnist also singled out for praise contractor Kenny Baldwin, who shut down his own construction business to devote 10-to-14-hour days, seven days a week, to the Broadway. Walt Madison, meanwhile, was described as "the Michelangelo of Broadway."

With the mayor and borough council due to arrive in gowns and tuxedos, Pitman's fire marshal had finally relented and given Slack Inc.'s Darrell Blood the theatre's certificate of occupancy. In return, Blood had to promise that all the electrical rewiring (now being completed for a second time to bring the theatre into code compliance) would be done within the next four weeks. "Basically, the electricians had to come back in, rip everything out and redo it all in 30 days, but they allowed us to open," remembers Blood.

Flowers had been donated by Merritt's House of Flowers (the same florist that had decorated the theatre for V.J. Day in 1945), Rose Bud Florist and Delaware Valley Wholesale Florists, the company started by the son and daughter-in-law of Ralph Wilkins, the Broadway's first owner-operator. Len Eckman Insurance – the agency later founded by the Pitman Grove Review columnist who'd once amusingly chronicled going hungry during the theatre's cooking schools – and Russ Johnson's Main Street Investments provided the evening's commemorative glassware.

Behind the Kimball organ, in formalwear was Nathan Figlio, now a second-generation Broadway organist. "The paint and carpet were fresh and the chandeliers were clean," remembers Figlio. "The theatre looked better than I'd seen it in my whole life." The benefit, with nearly 500 attendees, would raise much-needed money for the Broadway's operating expenses.

In the gala program, Broadway Theatre of Pitman President Peter Slack welcomed the assembled to "a celebration of the Broadway's revitalization. For Pitman, this event marks the rebirth of its theatre, long viewed as the focal point of our downtown business district." Both in the event program and on a large plaque hanging outside the theatre's second-floor lobby were the names of the hundreds of volunteers who had helped transform the theatre. On the adjoining wall was a photograph of Walt Madison, Kenny Baldwin and Wats Lohmann, identified as "The Broadway Boys." The theatre lights dimmed as Pitman High grad Jason Weber's 10-minute restoration documentary premiered for the gala crowd.

Among the celebrants was councilman Michael D. Batten Jr. and his wife, Bobbie. "Walking through the renovated theatre that night, you could see the possibilities," re-

Pitman Councilman Michael D. Batten Jr. and wife Bobbie at the reopening gala. Photo courtesy of Michael D. Batten Jr.

calls Michael. "I remember [councilman] Gene Shoemaker telling me at a council meeting, 'We need to become a destination.' With the restored Broadway Theatre, we could now do that. Peter Slack could have done anything with his money, but he chose to help the town. That 'what if?' question he used to ask himself while jogging past the theatre turned into 'I did.'"

Bill Lanning, who as a kid had attended the theatre's opening night in 1926, was delighted to be back inside the Broadway. "My dad was 6 or 7 when the theatre opened," says Susan Lanning Crispin. "It meant a lot for him to go back in his tux with my mom, Ruth, all decked out for the occasion. He was beaming that night. It made him so happy to see it revitalized. He was a Pitman person through and through." Bill Lanning would die five years later at 91.

Broadway owners Peter and Jill Slack at the 2006 reopening gala. Photo courtesy of the Slack family.

Cleanup volunteer James C. Brown also made a point of being at the gala. "It was incredibly exciting to see the theatre coming back into play," he remembers. Chamber of Commerce President Russ Johnson is more direct. "Everybody was out there with the red carpet, the velvet ropes, the spotlights crisscrossing in the sky and dressed to the nines. My first thought was, 'Holy shit, we're back. The town is back!'"

On Sept. 20, prior to the private gala, just as Ralph and Howard Wilkins had done 80 years earlier, Peter Slack and Darrell Blood opened the doors of the theatre for a public open house. This time, it was to reintroduce the town to its lovingly restored venue and provide a sneak preview of its 2007 inaugural mainstage Broadway musical season, featuring "Gypsy," "The Odd Couple," "Nunsense," "Disney's Beauty and the Beast," "Lend Me a Tenor" and "Oliver!" On

Broadway organist Nathan Figlio at the 2006 gala. Photo courtesy of Nathan Figlio.

hand for the occasion was one of Ralph Wilkins' old hires, former Broadway organist Robert M. Figlio, who for the first time got to hear his son Nathan playing the theatre's mighty Kimball organ. "At intermission, I remember seeing him in an opera box looking at me and beaming from ear to ear," Nathan recalls. It would be the only opportunity for Robert Figlio to hear the family's musical legacy live on at the Broadway. He died March 22, 2008, at age 69.

Across the street, the impact of the Broadway's reopening was already being felt. Pal Joey's Deli owner Joe Colli had to rush across the bridge to Philadelphia to grab 50 more loaves of bread to make hoagies for his crowd of customers. That same night, the local theatre troupe The Spotliters opened their production of the 1944 comedy "Harvey" on the refurbished Broadway stage. Sitting with his kids in the audience taking notes was Darrell Blood. "It was a good show, but they had sold maybe 40 tickets for the entire weekend run," remembers Blood. "That taught me an important lesson: My job is to put asses in seats."

Blood immediately set to work covering Pitman and neighboring towns with handbills promoting the Broadway's 2007 mainstage season and its bargain-basement $65 season price tag. Because they lacked the budget for postal mailings, Blood, Slack and their children had a new weekend activity.

"I have six children and with the exception of the 2-year-old, we were all out there for hours handing out flyers," recalls Blood. "We did that every weekend for a month or more." Remembers Blood's son Nicholas, who was 9 at the time: "I pulled this wagon full of the flyers and we'd run up to the houses, drop them off and then run back to the wagon for another pile." By the time the outreach campaign ended, Blood had won his side bet with his boss. While Peter Slack had predicted Blood could sign up 2,000 season subscribers, the outreach campaign had secured 6,000 subscribers for the inaugural theatrical season.

Blood's first star booking on the reopened Broadway stage was comedian George Carlin, who at 69 was no stranger to Pitman. The comic quickly sold out both of his October 2006 Broadway shows. While Carlin's often profane act might have seemed at odds with a town started as a Methodist summer camp, the opposite was true. The comic's relationship to Pitman and the Broadway stretched back decades; he'd performed sold-out shows there in 1987, 1989 and 1991. As he reasoned to the Times, "When you do 120 shows a year like I do, you get very creative in finding theatres. Pitman is a small town, but it's in the middle of a larger population area. I can go to a Pitman and I can still go into a Valley Forge Music Fair."

Displeased with the material in his last HBO special, Carlin was in the process of writing a new act. He decided to use the Broadway audience as an incubator for the material. He brought a white notepad onstage with him. At the back of the theatre was a stunned Darrell Blood. "He went on and started flipping the pages back and forth," says Blood. "I'm back there holding my head, thinking, 'This is our first big show and this guy is up there *reading* his act!' But the audience was eating it up." Blood wasn't the only one in the theatre sweating. Privately, Carlin was battling a case of the flu. Even under the weather, Carlin managed to wring a joke out of his condition. Blowing his nose onstage, Carlin slyly stuffed the used tissue into his pocket, waited a beat, then told the crowd, "eBay!" And because he knew his audiences in Pitman loved it, Carlin even dusted off his classic "seven dirty words" routine. The shows would be Carlin's final curtain call at the Broadway. He died of a heart attack on June 22, 2008.

Walt Madison remembers seeing a neighbor under the Broadway marquee out front after the show. "She said, 'Walt, wasn't that great? And the best part of all? It's right here.'"

On Friday, Jan. 12, 2007, the Broadway's new team was put to its first real test as the 1959 Jule Styne-Stephen Sondheim musical "Gypsy" kicked off the theatre's inaugural mainstage season. The near-capacity crowd included owner Peter Slack, who had delayed a business trip so he could attend the premiere. Gary Schneider was one of the house musicians that night playing in the very same 12-person orchestra pit used in 1926 by the first Broadway Orchestra. "We honestly didn't know how much work it would translate into for us," Schneider recalls. "We just knew the theatre was opening back up and we got called for a gig. I've now been here 18 years. Unlike a lot of other local theatres, the Broadway's support for using live musicians has never wavered. A lot of the guys playing with me in the pit in 2025 were there doing 'Gypsy' with me in 2007."

Playbill from the inaugural Broadway musical staged at the theatre. Courtesy of the Broadway Theatre.

Cast as Mama Rose, "Gypsy's" force-of-nature role, was actress Carol Furphy-Labinski. "Earning cheers from the audience is Carol Furphy-Labinski," wrote Courier-Post reviewer Robert Baxter. "Furphy-Labinski has a trumpet in her throat. She opens it impressively in Rose's big solos that bring both acts to a triumphant end." The Broadway's new subscribers were equally impressed. They promptly returned for the theatre's next production.

While live theatre at the Broadway was finding a foothold, the venue's experiment as a second-run movie house was sputtering, drawing anemic audiences even to crowd-pleasers like Sylvester Stallone's "Rocky Balboa." "We realized a single-screen just wasn't going to work when you have six, eight and ten screens all around us," explains Peter Slack. "For movies, we'd have 10 to 40 people. That's when we decided to focus on live performance."

With hundreds of people flowing back into the Broadway to see live theatre, two new restaurants emerged on Pitman's main street, including South Jersey restaurateur Robert Sanabria's Word of Mouth. Adding to the offerings, Peter and Jill Slack had debuted the 25-seat Stage Right Café a few doors down from the Broadway so theatre patrons could grab a cappuccino or an ice cream. "Before we opened, visitors couldn't enjoy a full night here because everything closes so early," explained Slack to the Gloucester County Times. "I wanted to meet the needs of our theatre customers and encourage even more people to come and enjoy downtown."

With multiple vacant storefronts on Broadway large enough for restaurants – including two former banks and the space that had housed Drissel's Hardware – decades-long public discourse over Pitman's storied status as a "dry town" began anew. "We actually had a restaurant say they wouldn't come because they can't offer drinks," Pitman Mayor Alice Polocz told the Times. "It's a good opportunity to make money."

The talk in town quickly spilled over to the Times letters page. "Why do I have to go out of town to have a glass of wine with a restaurant dinner? What if the town sold a couple of liquor licenses as restaurant-use only and were able to add a local tax on each drink sold, creating a continuous flow of revenue for the town?" wrote Pitman resident Jeff McNulla. Responded fellow Pitmanite L. Kramer, "We don't need liquor stores or restaurants that serve alcohol in Pitman. Let the alcohol lovers drive a mile or two to get their drinks. If that's too much trouble for them, let them do without. Alcohol is a poison. It's no good for anyone."

By the end of September 2007, Pitman Mayor Alice Polocz and the borough council had opted to put the choice to voters. "We decided that it was really not a decision that just six or seven members of the council should make," she explained, "but that the town should have a voice in it." Pitman remained one of five communities in South Jersey's Gloucester County without liquor licenses (although restaurants permitted BYOB). Glassboro, Pitman's neighboring town five minutes away, was home to Rowan University (formerly Glassboro State), a fast-growing campus. In a town perennially brimming with 21-year-olds, Glassboro had a host of alcohol-serving establishments and package stores.

According to the state division of Alcoholic Beverage Control, Pitman, with its population of 9,200, was eligible for three liquor consumption licenses and one package goods license. An unexpected bonus for Peter Slack and the Broadway Theatre? Under state law, if voters green-lighted alcohol sales, the theatre, as a performing arts space with more than 1,000 seats, would be allowed to serve spirits on show nights. Like the town's 1969 Sunday blue law referendum, the ballot initiative would be nonbinding.

"It's still going to attract a bar crowd and I don't see the benefit to it," Jack Lescure, the owner of Hero's restaurant on Broadway, told the Times. But resident Kristina Mortiz saw the issue differently. "I think the downtown would pick up, especially now that the theatre is open." Pitman United Methodist Church's Rev. Lanie B. Price weighed in by reading a reporter the Methodist Discipline: "We affirm our long-standing support of abstinence from alcohol as a faithful witness to God's liberating and redeeming love." When the Times reached out for his perspective, Broadway owner Peter Slack was diplomatic: "It would be positive … but the theatre has succeeded this far with the great support of the community both as volunteers, contributors and customers. Their voice regarding this issue is very important and therefore I look forward to learning the outcome of the ballot question."

On election night, Pitmanites didn't have to wait long for a verdict. Just as in the case of the 1969 Sunday blue law referendum, voters were overwhelmingly decisive. Not only did residents vote down the measure by 60 percent (1,787 no votes to 1,167 yes votes), but Democrats who had supported the measure, including Alice Polocz, the first woman elected Pitman mayor, were swept out of office. In as new mayor was Republican councilman Michael Batten Jr., along with two new Republican councilmen, Michael L. Razze Jr. and Russell C. Johnson III, former president of the Chamber of Commerce. The issue had clearly driven Pitmanites to the polls. "Usually we don't see this many voters unless it's a presidential election," said poll worker Eleanor Helverson.

From door knocking during the campaign, Mike Batten knew which way the wind was blowing on the referendum. "People were adamant about it," he recalls. "It became a focal point of the campaign. A lot of the older families were staunchly against it." Per New Jersey state mandate, the question could not be put back on the ballot for five years.

The final vote tally wasn't even in when Batten handed incoming councilman Russ Johnson a slip of paper outlining his economic development plan for Pitman's downtown. "When Peter Slack bought the theatre, the downtown woke up," explains Batten. "We were sitting on a gold mine in Pitman. We just had to figure out a way to mine it."

By the summer of 2009, with the success of its mainstage musical season, the Broadway Theatre of Pitman, as it was now professionally referred to, was turning a profit. Thanks to thousands of subscribers, the theatre was attracting crowds of 800 for each performance. Like Duffy Platt before them booking country acts, the theatre's new managing director, Pat Mangano and general manager Darrell Blood had hit upon a successful formula of staging crowd-favorite musicals that kept "asses in seats," as Blood described his job. In 2009, those hits included productions of "Annie Get Your Gun," Oklahoma!" and "Little Shop of Horrors," mixed with more adventurous fare like "All Shook Up," a show mashing up the songs of Elvis Presley with a plot based on William Shakespeare's "Twelfth Night."

Drew Molotsky first came onboard at the Broadway in 2009 to direct his first musical. He's been back every year since. "I wholeheartedly believe it's the best place to work in the region," Molotsky explains. "It's a beautiful space in which to create theatre and we get exceptional support and resources from the theatre itself because of the huge subscription base. And because you get audiences of 600 to 800 people per show, actors want to perform there. That's why we get a higher level of talent auditioning."

Among the new talent onstage in 2009 was Heather Mattingley Grasso, taking to the air in the lead role of "Peter Pan," thanks to a flying rig system. Like Molotsky, Grasso decided she liked the view in Pitman. She would go on to perform as Bombalurina in "Cats" and Polly in "Crazy for You." In 2018, she earned accolades from The Philadelphia Inquirer when Molotsky asked her to do the choreography for "Chicago."

Adds Broadway Theatre of Pitman mainstage actor and director Kyrus Keenan Westcott: "I've been doing theatre for a long time and all of the people behind the scenes there make it an enjoyable experience every single time." Over the years, Westcott has witnessed a lot of evolution both on and offstage. When he first started performing at the venue in 2013, Westcott was usually one of only two or three people of color in the cast. Additionally, he sometimes had challenges getting to and from the theatre. "I got pulled over by police more in Pitman than in any other town," Westcott recalls. "This happened six times. You know how many tickets I received? Zero. I loved the theatre, but I used to hate driving there. I always had to be careful. Thankfully, things have changed."

The Broadway stage had also instituted a popular Saturday-morning children's theatre series (to help ensure the next generation of mainstage subscribers), a children's summer theatre camp and an annual family-friendly holiday stage show. "It all made sense," reflects Blood. "Live theatre, live entertainment, children's shows, children's theatre summer camp. It all meshes together. The audiences feed off of one another." Adds owner Peter Slack: "Thanks to Darrell's management, we were making money. Keep in mind, Darrell is the CFO of our medical publishing company. He had to jump in and start negotiating the rights to Broadway shows and sometimes deal with slimy talent agents. This was a whole new world. Not only did Darrell learn this world, he's become a leader in it."

Among the participants in the summer children's theatre camp was 9-year-old Pitman native Keith David Brown, who had seen his first movie, Pixar's "Finding Nemo," at the Broadway in 2003 and met the Munchkins at the 2004 sing-along screening of "The Wizard of Oz." Brown was cast as dad Pongo in the summer camp production of "101 Dalmatians" and, later, as Belle's father Maurice in "Beauty and the Beast." Now a Rowan University film student, Brown reflects with a laugh: "For whatever reason, I was giving off paternal vibes. Even though he was the dad, I was surprised by how relatively few lines Pongo had. I had more fun playing crazy old Maurice, especially since he had more lines than Pongo!"

2006 Broadway restoration team: Walter Madison, Watson Lohmann and Ken Baldwin.

The Broadway Theatre's success had translated into 118,000 people visiting Pitman annually. A sixth restaurant in Uptown Pitman (as the town's marketing folks were now calling the business district) was about to open. As he and his wife, Bobbie, ate out in neighboring communities, Mayor Mike Batten was busy putting down his business card while talking up the business district's rebirth. "When a restaurant owner hears there are 800 people who want to have dinner before a play, that's very inviting," the mayor told The Philadelphia Inquirer as he cut a customer's hair at Joe's Barber Shop.

While Pitman's newly christened Uptown continued to attract new restaurants that could offer only BYOB options to diners, changes were afoot in Trenton. In 2012, New Jersey Gov. Chris Christie signed a series of laws intended to help the growth of the state's wineries and craft beer makers. New Jersey's beer industry in particular had lagged behind that of its neighbors in New York, Pennsylvania and Delaware. The new legislation allowed craft breweries to sell their beer on premises as part of a brewery tour. No liquor license was required, as the products would be manufactured on site. In a separate bill to support the state's 48 wineries, Christie had signed legislation allowing them to sell directly to consumers and retailers. The initiative had been one of the most embattled bills of the 2011 state legislative session. The new law also allowed wineries to partner with restaurants to sell directly to diners without a liquor license. By 2012, New Jersey was being recognized as one of the top wine-producing states in the country.

The new laws would forever alter Pitman's identity as a "dry town" founded on Methodist church doctrine.

By fall 2014, two restaurants in Pitman, the Bus Stop Music Café and Venice, were taking advantage of the new consumer wine law. The development did not go unnoticed on the editorial page of the South Jersey Times: "Will wonders never cease? Wine is to be sold in dry-as-dust Pitman? A bemused borough council has shown no inclination to challenge the practice, which, in effect, grants these eateries a de facto liquor license." Privately, however, Mike Batten was seething. "We had voted on alcohol and then the state steps in and says, 'OK, you can do this.' I felt like our citizens took a slap to the face."

Two doors down from the Bus Stop Music Café, budding craft beer brewers Justin Fleming, his wife, Jeannette and friend Dave Domanski were eyeing an empty storefront. Seizing on the momentum of the state's craft beer law, the trio decided to open Kelly Green Brewing Company, the first-ever brewery in Pitman's nearly 110-year history. The business would feature "eight to 10 taps full of homegrown craft beer right from the heart of Pitman," previewed Justin Fleming. Kelly Green would also offer sales of 64-ounce growlers that patrons could purchase and take to any BYOB restaurant in town.

While the news upset the town's traditional churchgoing crowd, younger craft beer connoisseurs welcomed the development. Another thing working in the new microbrewery's favor – Justin and Jeannette Fleming were not outsiders. Both had been born and raised in Pitman and were raising their daughter in the house where Justin had grown up. The Flemings' business approvals were unanimously green-lighted by the borough's planning and zoning board. "This is our home and we know the history of the town," Justin Fleming explained to the Times. "We know that the town is very religious ... but we thought it was time to revitalize a little and we're very excited for the chance to do this." Pitman's new mayor, Russell Johnson, who had successfully run for borough council in 2007 opposing the alcohol referendum, acknowledged the impact the new state laws were having in Pitman. "We need to support these businesses," said Johnson. "This will be new and different."

When Bus Stop Music Café owner Vic Martinson decided to retire and vacate his decade-old restaurant two doors from the new brewery, Megan Myers and Emily Barnes announced they would be taking over the space to open Human Village Brewing Company, Pitman's second microbrewery. Instead of competition, Barnes told the Times, she envisioned the pair of breweries steps from each other as a destination. "We've driven hours to go to breweries," she said. "We think with all of the shore traffic," the location would be ideal. Added John Fitzpatrick, now Pitman Chamber president: "They are going to bring a younger crowd and I think we can build on that. It will be a catalyst so you can come, try some beer and have some dinner and then maybe stay at the bed-and-breakfast." The plan also intrigued Philadelphia Inquirer "Joe Sixpack" columnist Don Russell, executive director of the Garden State Craft Brewers Guild. He envisioned "a veritable brewery row in a borough where for 100 years, the closest thing to a stiff drink was a bottle of hair tonic at the barber shop."

And so at 11:30 a.m. on May 7, 2016, Pitman Mayor Russ Johnson cut the grand-opening ribbon at Kelly Green Brewing, officially proclaiming Pitman to be "damp." "We couldn't be more excited. It's going to be a big shot in the arm for this town."

With wine and beer now freely flowing in town, with zero alcohol-tax revenue backwashing into the borough's coffers, Pitman residents could see the inevitable heading down Broadway. On Nov. 8, 2016, a second alcohol referendum was placed on the ballot. The potential seismic shift attracted the attention of Philadelphia Inquirer columnist Kevin Riordan, who walked along Broadway to talk to business owners. The initiative "may well save this town," said Anthony Asbury, owner of Sweet Lula's restaurant. "The naysayers are dying off. Young people are moving to Pitman and saying, 'We think it's time for a change.'" Pitman restaurateur Vito Mannino, who owned the white-tablecloth Mannino's Cucina Italiana, agreed. "A lot of people were against [the brewery]," he reasoned. "The talk of the town was, 'Oh, my God, we're going to have all these drunks,' but it's been very successful and no trouble at all."

Jane McCausland, a fourth-generation Pitmanite and chair of the Pitman Historical Museum, wanted to preserve the town's traditions. "Being a dry town is part of the DNA of Pitman," she told Riordan. And even though his Broadway Theatre stood to benefit thanks to the state's built-in license to sell alcohol for 1,000-seat arts venues, owner Peter Slack remained diplomatic. While he conceded that as a resident he had already voted yes "because it makes sense economically," if the measure crashed and burned again at the ballot box, he predicted, "the town is going to do just fine."

Unlike in 2007, this time Pitmanites voted overwhelmingly in favor of the initiative by over 65 percent, with 2,935 residents voting for it while 1,604 were opposed. Voters had decided alcohol could now legally be served in a town founded in 1905 as the outgrowth of a Methodist camp meeting site in the Pitman Grove. A borough where a 1912 stone Women's Christian Temperance Union water fountain still stood downtown in Ballard Park (albeit in use as a flower box for petunias planted by the Pitman Garden Club).

In retrospect, Russ Johnson sees the state's legislative beer and wine allowances "as a series of transitional steps that made people more comfortable. The demographics of the town had shifted dramatically from 2007 to 2016. In 2016, I wasn't hearing the same kind of resistance from residents that I had heard in 2007."

Down at the Broadway, Peter Slack had acquired 47 S. Broadway, the property next door, to relieve an increasingly urgent need, a byproduct of the larger crowds now visiting the venue. "We bought the building primarily to install bathrooms," says Slack with a laugh. "I don't know what happened in 1926, but today's habits require more bathrooms!" To fill the rest of the space, Peter and Jill Slack decided to move their Stage Right concept into the space, rebranding it as a wine bar.

The town's evolving attitudes didn't surprise Warren Carr, who had been observing life in Pitman for 80 years. "There were enough people who enjoyed a drink to support the passage of the referendum," Carr reflects. "Pitman was changing. It wasn't just the old-fashioned Methodists living there anymore." Explains former Pitman councilman Kevin Austin: "The worst-kept secret was that Pitman had the most basement bars per capita of any town in Gloucester County." Adds Carr: "People just didn't want to talk about it. When I was growing up, we had a speakeasy on Simpson Avenue down the street from our house. Everybody in town knew it was there, but nobody wanted to blow the whistle. The beer truck used to come there and deliver, for God's sake. It wasn't any secret."

While some longtime Pitman residents still bristled at the idea that spirits would soon be served on Broadway just steps from where Scripture had been studied at summer Methodist camp revivals, the referendum's passage had one unexpected dividend. Like the town's now-thriving iconic 1926 theatre, another long-abandoned Broadway landmark was about to be jolted back to life, adding even more cylinders to the town's humming economic engine.

View from the balcony in the restored Broadway Theatre.
Photo courtesy of the Slack family.

Miss Pitman 1999 Erica Scanlon Harr in "Always, Patsy Cline." Photo by Joe Grasso. Courtesy of the Broadway Theatre.

CHAPTER ELEVEN

"Please take care of yourself and your loved ones."

2018–2024

On the evening of Oct. 10, 2018, protesters were back on Broadway. But this time, the person causing the commotion inside the theatre was fully clothed. Sitting onstage in a purple print dress, right-wing firebrand Ann Coulter was in conversation with 1210 WPHT Philadelphia conservative talk radio host Chris Stigall discussing her new book "Resistance Is Futile! How the Trump-Hating Left Lost Its Collective Mind."

Earlier in the evening, Coulter fans arriving at the event lined the sidewalk in front of the theatre and engaged in shouting matches with protesters across the street, some of whom were members of Rowan University's College Democrats group. The protesters waved "Resistance Is Never Futile" signs. Other Pitmanites held aloft "Hate Has No Place In Pitman" banners. As a Coulter supporter wearing an American flag bandanna tied around his head stood under the theatre marquee, a man across the street shouted, "Take that flag off your head. It's disrespectful!" as another protester added, "Hate speech is anti-American."

Inside, each attendee received a copy of Coulter's book during the evening's lively interview and Q&A session. Later, Pitman councilwoman Amy Rudley praised the town's police and fire departments for the "wonderful job" ensuring the evening remained orderly. Rudley added to NJ Advance Media, "Protests are a part of our nation's history and our freedoms. The protests and the counter-protesters were peaceful, with no violence or significant issues."

A year later, the response to the Coulter book-signing would seem sedate when it was announced the Broadway would host a daylong conference. Sponsored by Minds, a cryptocurrency social media platform, "Combating Racism and Violence" sounded innocuous enough. But when the list of speakers began being disseminated online, reaction quickly shifted. Among those on the schedule: Carl Benjamin, a right-wing U.K. Independence Party member, whose YouTube channel had recently been demonetized after he told a female Labour Party member, "I wouldn't even rape you ... feminism is cancer." Another participant, Mark Meechan, had been found guilty of a hate crime in the U.K. after teaching his girlfriend's pug to do a Nazi salute and posting a video of it on YouTube. Members of No Hate New Jersey took to social media to denounce the event.

First, the theatre received a flurry of angry phone calls and the Broadway Theatre's Twitter account got hacked. Then came the threats, including one promising to burn down the 92-year-old landmark. Working with the Pitman Police Department to trace the origin of the threats, Mayor Russ Johnson told The Philadelphia Inquirer, "That's the stuff I won't tolerate." Broadway general manager Darrell Blood then released a statement to the press: "After discussions with the event organizer, it was mutually agreed that the event would no longer be held at the Broadway Theatre in Pitman." Mayor Johnson explained that while he supported the right to free speech for both sides, the proposed event had blemished his 2.3-square-mile town. "We have other things to deal with," Johnson said.

For Johnson, one of those other priorities included a potential economic renewal project down the street at 106 S. Broadway. In 1907, Alcyon Park owner George Carr and his physician brother Henry Carr had spearheaded the creation of the town's first bank. After outgrowing its original location in the rear of Dilks' Drug Store, a lavish new building at 106 S. Broadway was erected in 1911. George Carr would go on to serve as its first president, with Mayor Joseph M. McCowan as vice president and a young up-and-comer named Wadsworth Cresse brought in as bank cashier.

But for the past decade, the beautiful granite Pitman National Bank & Trust had sat hulled out and vacant.

Among those disheartened by the building's state of disrepair was Warren Carr, whose father, George W. Carr Jr., had been named for George Carr. Beginning in 1967, under the shingle Cresse and Carr, Counsellors at Law, Warren Carr would build a successful practice in Woodbury with the son of Pitman National's first cashier, Wadsworth Cresse Jr. "The bank had survived the Great Depression, thanks to what some characterized as George Carr's 'stinginess,'" recounts Carr. "I don't know that it was necessarily stingy, but it allowed the bank to survive."

Now abandoned after being gutted by a property flipper who'd gone bust in the 2008 economic downturn, the structure was once again owned by the Borough of Pitman. Brandon Hedenberg, a young real estate broker and developer working in his hometown, toured the structure with a prospective buyer. "Water and outside elements had gotten into the building and there was a gaping hole in the floor," he recalls. Hedenberg's client beat a hasty retreat from the disintegrating property. "Historic value aside," Hedenberg says, "it was going to be a real project."

Then one night Pitman Mayor Russ Johnson bumped into Broadway business owner William K. Merryman on the sidewalk outside borough hall. When Johnson casually floated the idea of redeveloping the hulking granite building next door, Merryman's eyes lit up. His roots in Pitman extended back to the 1920s, when his grandmother Florence Merryman had attended Methodist summer camp meetings in the Pitman Grove. He had purchased the building that housed Merritt's House of Flowers, later adding other Pitman properties to his portfolio.

Vito G. Mannino, the restaurateur who operated Pizzeria Mannino's and Mannino's Cucina Italiana in buildings owned by Merryman on Broadway, was also intrigued. The duo decided to partner on a British pub concept, which would require the issuance of Pitman's first-ever alcohol license. But touring the space for the first time gave Merryman pause. "There had been a fire in there at some point," recalls Merryman. "The day I went to look at the building, I'm standing inside and rain is coming in on my head. A good portion of the roof was gone. We had no idea if it was even going to remain standing. Vito and I would look at each other and ask, 'What are we doing?!'"

The gutted 1911 Pitman National Bank & Trust in 2018. Photo courtesy of Bill Merryman.

Mayor Russ Johnson became the redevelopment project's head cheerleader. He had worked at the bank in 1998 when it was a First Fidelity branch and had affection for the structure. But he also knew what an economic boost the building could bring to Broadway if resuscitated.

At its Sept. 11, 2018, council meeting, the Borough of Pitman authorized a letter of intent for Merryman and Mannino to occupy and develop the bank building: "We want to thank Bill and Vito for their vision and passion for this building and for continuing their investment in our Uptown." To mark the historic occasion, the restaurateurs posed for a photo with Mayor Johnson holding a mockup of their Merryman's Pub coat of arms logo.

Originally, Merryman and Mannino applied for a concessionaire's permit with the state's Alcoholic Beverage Control department and planned to lease the property from the borough. Inspired by a recent trip to London, Merryman had a U.K.-style red telephone booth shipped to the front of the building. It immediately became the number one social media selfie station in Pitman. "Suddenly, there were pictures all over Facebook," Merryman recalls. "People loved it."

Inside the 1911 bank, as safes were being hauled away and coolers were being installed, another discovery was made. The building had no gas or water lines. "They literally had to close off and dig up Broadway to run water and gas lines to the building," says Merryman.

As Mannino and Merryman sank more and more money into reviving the structure, they decided they wanted to own the building ("It was about being able to control our destiny," explains Merryman). A deal was struck with the borough – the bank would be sold to the pair for one dollar in exchange for their financing the renovation and purchasing Pitman's first liquor license. By the time the last bar stool was installed and the final flat-screen TV hung, the pair had sunk an estimated $1.2 million dollars into building out Pitman's first-ever pub.

"It was the hardest thing that I've ever done," Mannino told 08071 magazine. "But we were able to complete the building and keep the structure intact." Added Merryman: "Everyone told me that we were a bit crazy ... but I've always been a bit of a dreamer." On the restaurant side, Mannino was busy creating a pub-style menu, including panko-crusted fish and chips, Guinness and short rib pot pie, brick-oven flatbreads, barbeque pulled-pork macaroni and cheese and cheesesteak egg rolls. By March 2020, with a gleaming gold Merryman's Pub "Eat, Drink & Be Merry" sign greeting drivers at the corner of Broadway and Pitman Avenue, food was being delivered in anticipation of the pub's grand opening, set for March 17, St. Patrick's Day.

And then Covid struck.

"Everything was ready to rock 'n' roll and bam, everything shuts down," remembers Russ Johnson. "Here we had these two guys taking the building from a shell to what it became and then having the rug pulled out from under them." Adds Bill Merryman: "You invest all that money and then we were dead in the water before we even opened. On a good day in this business, you have no idea if you're going to be successful. Most restaurants don't make it. And now this?"

Down the street at the Broadway, with Sunday shows on March 16 at 2 and 7 p.m., the theatre's staging of the 1963 musical "She Loves Me" was wrapping up its third weekend of performances. At the Kimball organ, Nathan Figlio, an autoimmune-compromised 30-year ER nurse, was masked. "It was a subdued audience," Figlio remembers. "The crowd was smaller. It wasn't our typical house. People were there to have a good time, but the world was not normal."

While surveying the worsening coronavirus headlines, hard decisions were being made. After a conversation with Walnut Street Theatre artistic director Bernard Havard across the river in Philadelphia, Darrell Blood, the Broadway's general manager, made the call to cancel the remaining weekend of "She Loves Me." Also nixed was the theatre's next mainstage show, "Big River," which had been scheduled for April 17 to May 10. At the bottom of its March 17, 2020, Facebook post announcing the cancellations, the Broadway told patrons: "Please take care of yourself and your loved ones. We look forward to seeing you at the theatre very soon!"

For theatregoers from the Pitman Country era, the Broadway's response to the pandemic demonstrated that Darrell Blood was no Clayton Platt. Unlike Platt, who'd held onto the cash from Pitman Country advance ticket sales after acts canceled, Blood promptly returned the full cost of "Big River" tickets to patrons. Later, when the Broadway had to cancel the three remaining shows of the 2020 season, he sent a followup check to subscribers with the remainder of their season refund. "The big question was how long we would be able to continue without producing a show," remembers Broadway marketing manager Nicholas Blood. "Especially when we had to issue refund checks. We had put that money aside and suddenly we had to give all of that money back."

In response, many Pitmanites decided to exemplify the town slogan "The Small Town With a Big Heart." "A good amount of our season subscribers called or emailed to tell us they weren't going to cash their refund checks," recalls Nick Blood. "They wanted to donate the money back to the theatre to help us out through this tough time."

Reminiscent of Ralph Wilkins going to work for his father Howard at Green's Opera House in Woodbury 100 years earlier, Nick Blood was one of Darrell Blood's six children who had grown up in the theatre. Nick was 9 when the Broadway celebrated its grand reopening in 2006 and all through high school he had worked on the stage crew, building and painting sets for the mainstage shows. After majoring in marketing and accounting at Rutgers University, Nick decided to join what was becoming the family business. Nick's brother Michael worked in the theatre's sound booth as the Broadway's technical director.

In the early weeks of the pandemic, it was eerie for Pitman Mayor Michael L. Razze Jr. to step out into the middle of Broadway. "There wasn't a single car on the road," says

Razze. "At various points in my life, you could look downtown and not see anything happening on Broadway. But in 2020, our downtown economic boom was in full swing. It was unsettling and surreal." From a laptop on his back porch, Razze met with the borough council on Zoom to discuss ways they could help local businesses while providing updates on infections, deaths and recoveries to residents on the borough's Facebook page. After the state and then the borough signed off on takeout alcohol, Michael and Tammy Razze quietly celebrated their 25th wedding anniversary on their back porch with cocktails and dinner acquired from downtown businesses.

In late June, the Broadway Theatre's 25-member staff had to be laid off. Among those furloughed was the mainstage music coordinator, Gary Schneider, who oversaw the musicians and the arrangements for the theatre's musicals. "It was a scary time for sure," Schneider recalls. "We had no idea what was going to happen. People didn't know when they would work again." Meanwhile, a federal Covid small business grant helped keep the 94-year-old building running and also financed repair projects, including reupholstering the downstairs seats while the theatre sat idle.

Heather Mattingley Grasso, who had debuted on the Broadway stage in 2009 as an actor in "Peter Pan," was now the mainstage's producing artistic director. During the lockdown, she kept in touch with the theatre's creative team and its roster of actors. "I was part mom and cheerleader," Grasso recalls. "I kept telling them, 'When we come back … '. They needed to know it was going to be OK." In the interim, Grasso stayed busy at the theatre, overseeing the installation of a new Marley dance floor in the studio and the renovation of the green room bathrooms.

By summer 2020, Merryman's Pub, housed in the now completely remodeled 1911 Pitman National Bank, had opened its doors to the public. It wasn't the champagne-popping debut that Bill Merryman or Vito Mannino had envisioned, but Merryman's was finally open, mostly for take-out orders. And thanks to Pitman borough council, which had retained ownership of the old bank parking lot behind the pub, Merryman's was permitted to erect tents for socially distanced outdoor dining. The town had also expanded the dining footprint out front and allowed alcohol to be served alfresco, the first-ever cocktails sold with a liquor license in the town's 115-year history. Other eateries like Pitman's venerable Chinese restaurant Ming Lok and Attilio's Pizza & Pasta were limping along doing takeout. In Ballard Park, picnic tables had been relocated to the green space to create a designated public eating area so residents could gather outside.

The former 1911 Pitman National Bank is now Merryman's Pub, Pitman's first full-service bar.

But with no shows booked at the Broadway, most of Uptown Pitman's diners were local residents out for a walk with their kids and pets, attempting to stave off stir-craziness at home. By Labor Day weekend, with some restrictions now lifted, the theatre's general manager, Darrell Blood, was willing to try an experiment. He reached out to Vinny Adinolfi, founder of The Bronx Wanderers, the retro rock act that had become a favorite with Broadway audiences. Would the group be interested in playing five socially distanced shows with masked audiences limited to 75? As it turns out, Vinny and the boys, usually a mainstay act in Las Vegas, were available. On Sept. 4-6, 2020, the Broadway's doors were back open — with 6-foot social distancing requirements, spaced seating and temperature checks. Tickets could be purchased at the door for $20. "We gave it a shot," says Nick Blood, "but ultimately, it wasn't viable."

The Broadway stage went dark once again.

Darrell Blood had now returned about $1 million in advance ticket sales to Broadway patrons. Meanwhile, it was costing Peter Slack about $300 a day to keep the utilities on and maintain the 95-year-old theatre. Then came an unpleasant but necessary conversation between Slack, his CFO/theatre general manager Blood and the Slack company attorney. "Basically, he told us that with shutdown and the return of a million dollars to subscribers, if I wanted to donate the theatre, there wouldn't be any tax benefit — it was essentially worthless," recalls Slack. "It was the same scenario if I wanted to sell it. It was over. Darrell wasn't booking shows, the theatre was dark and all we were doing was paying heating bills."

The attorney then suggested one prospective path forward: If Slack and Blood wanted to take the time, reopen the Broadway and rebuild the theatre's subscriber base, then Slack would be able to sell or donate his investment. Peter Slack turned to his CFO and asked a pivotal question: "Are you up for round two?"

Down the street, positive word-of-mouth spread among locals about Pitman's first full-service bar, Merryman's Pub. Ironically, the pub was across the street from the 1912 Women's Christian Temperance Union fountain. The pub also stood just feet away from the First Avenue arched entrance to the Pitman Grove, where Merryman's grandmother once strolled to Bible study. "My mother jokes that my grandmother would be rolling in her grave knowing the family name was attached to Pitman's first pub!" Bill Merryman laughs. "My grandfather Guy might have been a little bit more understanding. I'm told he occasionally took a sip or two."

Just across the street from the pub is McCowan Memorial Library, named after Pitman's first mayor, Joseph M. McCowan, who became Pitman National Bank's second president in 1935, succeeding George Carr. The library was a favorite place for Merryman's father, Ken, a history professor. The elder Merryman had died in 2004 at age 73. Ken Merryman's favorite reading nook now overlooked the town's popular new gathering place run by his son and bearing his name. "My dad and I always talked about opening a business in Pitman together," recalls Merryman. "He loved Pitman. He got sick and ultimately it didn't happen. The pub is my way of honoring him and our family and doing something for the town he loved." Warren Carr is delighted the building his family helped erect was saved. "I'm sorry that it's no longer used as a bank," says Carr. "But I certainly don't mind it being used for a pizza parlor restaurant, either, especially since I've had the pleasure of eating their pizza. It's a worthy addition to Broadway."

By the summer of 2021, with 67 percent of the United States population having received at least one dose of the new Covid vaccine, parking on Broadway was once again becoming a problem as sidewalk dining surged. Pitman native Carmen Cattafi was among those enjoying the novelty of patronizing the town's first pub. "Standing outside Merryman's Pub with an alcoholic beverage in my hand was something I thought I'd never see," Cattafi concedes with a laugh. "It was a big change for Pitman. The world did not end. But Pitman did become much more appealing for people, both in and from out of town." Kevin Austin, who served on the borough council when the liquor referendum passed in 2016, was happy to see the town finally benefiting from alcohol tax revenue. "We had been trying to keep the tax rate down," explains Austin. "It made sense. When I was a paperboy delivering the Evening Bulletin in town, I took my two dollars a week and deposited it at the Pitman National Bank. Now you can order a beer there. Times change."

As the business district slowly came back to life, Carmen Cattafi saw his Merryman's pint glass as half-full. "People patronized the restaurants and stores on Broadway to keep them afloat so our neighbors who had put their hearts and souls into these small businesses wouldn't close down." Adds Mayor Michael Razze: "With the theatre closed, the community came together to support our businesses. Even if it was just grabbing takeout, it kept things going when our businesses couldn't operate traditionally."

In 2019, mirroring the award bestowed on Ralph Wilkins in 1966, the Pitman Chamber of Commerce had honored Broadway owner Peter Slack with its Lifetime Service Award. And now, like Ralph Wilkins in 1969 fighting for Sunday hours to keep the Broadway afloat, Slack decided to explain his economic realities to the borough council. Unless he had a dedicated revenue source when the pandemic ended, the theatre might not reopen.

Under state law, given the size of its population, Pitman was eligible to issue a second liquor license.

Consequently, the Broadway's owner was among those addressing council asking to be considered for the town's second alcohol permit. Converting his wine bar adjacent to the theatre into a full-service bar and restaurant could be the solution to getting the Broadway back into the black.

"My biggest fear was, Peter and his organization were going to say that they were tired of spending money to keep the theatre going without a clear picture of how they were going to recover from this," recalls Mayor Michael Razze. "And if Peter Slack, the local guy, walks away, will we lose that crown jewel and all of the economic progress we've made along with it?"

For Mayor Razze, it came down to one question: "What do we need to do within the scope of our authority to stop that from happening?" The borough council listened to all the prospective bidders and later accepted three bids for the borough's second liquor license. The minimum set by the borough was $301,000. The winning bid came in at $430,000. It was Peter Slack's. Still, with Covid disruptions, it would take months for the state of New Jersey to sign off. And finally, since the new restaurant and bar would be located within the town's historic district, the Pitman Historic Commission would have to green-light the project.

With shots now in arms across the country and a revenue-producing lifeline on the way, producing artistic director Heather Mattingley Grasso and her team met up on Zoom to discuss how quickly they could get a musical back onstage. The answer came in the form of the two-person show "Always, Patsy Cline," starring hometown girl and Miss Pitman 1999 Erica Scanlon Harr in the title role. The theatre, now allowed to open to 400 masked audience members, scheduled six performances. On its Instagram account the theatre announced: "LIVE ENTERTAINMENT IS BACK AT THE BROADWAY THEATRE OF PITMAN!!!! We heard from our subscribers loud and clear. They can't wait any longer to enjoy a beautiful night out at the Broadway."

On July 9, 2021, for the first time in 16 long months, the Broadway Theatre of Pitman was back in business. Audiences flocked to "Always, Patsy Cline," so the Broadway immediately booked an encore production — the off-Broadway girl group musical "The Marvelous Wonderettes." For Pitmanites of a certain age, the show evoked their own small-town prom night memories spent at the theatre. Set in 1958 at the fictitious Springfield High School prom, "four girls with hopes and dreams as big as their crinoline skirts" belted out pop classics, including "Stupid Cupid" and "Lipstick on Your Collar." In between mainstage shows, the Broadway's summer camp for kids was selling out.

Keeping an eye on increasing Covid vaccinations and decreasing infection rates, the Broadway decided to go big for the fall of 2021. A casting call went out for Jonathan Larson's iconic musical "Rent." Fully vaccinated performers were asked to submit video auditions for the 16-cast-member show. Grasso and her assistant, Krystina Hawkinson (who like Grasso had started at the BTOP as a performer), immediately began sifting through dozens of emailed auditions.

Broadway organist Nathan Figlio was excited to be back behind the Kimball organ but had concerns about the 95-year-old pipe instrument's condition after sitting unplayed for 16 months. "When I fired it back up, there were only one or two cipher cycles [a pipe playing when it's not supposed to], but then it went right back to normal. It's an incredibly reliable instrument."

For many of the masked patrons in the audience, seeing "Rent" was an emotional experience. The musical, set in New York City's East Village in the 1990s at the height of the AIDS epidemic, was based on Puccini's opera "La Boheme," whose heroine Mimi perishes from tuberculosis at the final curtain. But in Larson's modern rock retelling, Mimi survives. Brought in to oversee the production was longtime Broadway Theatre of Pitman director Drew Molotsky. "At that moment in time, the world was starved for live theatre," he remembers. "We had the advantage of feeding the hungry."

On opening night, just before the audience filed in, organist Nathan Figlio, a longtime trauma nurse, addressed the cast, telling them how important this project was. Remembers "Rent" director Molotsky: "He spoke about his experiences as a younger man treating AIDS patients and the confluence of the pandemic and the AIDS epidemic. It was an incredibly moving moment."

"Telling that story, especially as the world was coming out of Covid, was incredibly powerful," says actor Kyrus Keenan Westcott, who portrayed Collins in the production. "We had no idea if people would show up. I really credit 'Rent' with helping the community feel comfortable with the theatre staging those types of shows." Adds artistic director Heather Mattingley Grasso: "'Seasons of Love' just punched everyone in the heart. Going through a tragedy like Covid, suddenly no one knew how much time they had left. It was a unifying, perfect show to come back with."

The Broadway's strategy worked. Hundreds of theatre patrons arrived for the two weekends of performances. "The pandemic was transformative in a lot of ways," says Molotsky. "'Rent' was not a subscription show because we didn't have a season to subscribe to. We were starting with a clean slate. 'Rent' provided a litmus test. We were thrilled when that theatre began filling up again."

Over Thanksgiving weekend, Broadway regulars also flooded back to see favorites The Bronx Wanderers, this time to robust crowds.

Thanks to Grasso and other returning furloughed staffers, an ambitious six-musical 2022 season was booked, with the Covid-delayed "Matilda" back in play, along with "The Sound of Music," "Pippin," "Disney's Beauty and the Beast," "Bright Star" and "Something Rotten." To entice potential subscribers, season tickets were dropped to $50 for all six shows. Remembers Broadway marketing manager Nick Blood: "It was a complete cross-our-fingers-and-hope situation. We had no idea if people would even leave their house." The Broadway Theatre of Pitman didn't have to wait long for an answer. So many advance subscriptions poured in, the theatre ended up surpassing its pre-Covid 2020 mainstage numbers.

On Feb. 17, 2022, Peter and Jill Slack welcomed the public to their new restaurant concept adjacent to the theatre – Martini's on Broadway. For classic film fans, Martini's was instantly recognizable as George Bailey's favorite Bedford Falls watering hole in the 1946 Frank Capra film "It's a Wonderful Life." Martini's featured black-and-white stills of former Broadway performers, including Jackie Gleason, Abbott and Costello and Mickey Rooney, on its walls, bookending a large photo of Jimmy Stewart sidled up at Martini's. In the front window was guardian angel Clarence Odbody's inscription to George inside his copy of "The Adventures of Tom Sawyer": "Remember, no man is a failure who has friends." At the entrance door was a large photograph of Johnny Cash, poised for action with his guitar.

In addition to an extensive martini and craft cocktail menu, Martini's on Broadway offered pre-theatre or post-theatre patrons shareable plates, including duck meatballs, a shrimp scampi flatbread and Brazilian steak with chimichurri sauce. "Just like the theatre, none of us had ever run a restaurant and bar before either," explains Peter Slack. "We had fits and starts and like any startup business, Martini's didn't make money the first day."

During the 2022 and 2023 holiday seasons, the restaurant even hosted "It's a Wonderful Night at Martini's on Broadway" movie trivia events, complete with a four-course dinner. Jeff Sanders, Pitman Economic Development Committee founding member and local Bedford Falls expert, developed the questions. Among the expert-level puzzlers: "What was the address of the old Granville house where George and Mary spent their wedding night?" (Answer: 320 Sycamore.)

On the Broadway mainstage, the inroads made by producing "Rent" had set the stage for Lin-Manuel Miranda's "In the Heights." In spring 2023, for the first time in the theatre's 97-year history, a show would be performed onstage with only black and brown performers — in a town with 92.3 percent white residents. Helming the show was veteran BTOP performer and director Kyrus Keenan Westcott, who had been introduced to the Broadway (and Pitman's police department) when he was cast in "Hairspray" in 2013. "Now we were doing a hip-hop musical in Pitman, N.J., with no white people in it," recalls Westcott. "We had no idea what the reaction would be. But like the theatre itself, Pitman has grown a lot over the years."

The cast of the 2023 production of "In the Heights." Photo by Nick Flagg. Courtesy of the Broadway Theatre.

Still, on opening night, Westcott was anxious sitting in the audience. "I told the cast just to focus on telling the story. There's a line from one of Aaron Burr's songs in 'Hamilton' where he sings, 'I am the one thing in life I can control.' That's what I passed on to the cast. 'We can't control what people think of us; the only thing we have control over is ourselves.'" For two-and-a-half hours, as Lin-Manuel Miranda's musical about Washington Heights, the close-knit community where he grew up, played out on-stage, Westcott waited. In the show's final moments, bodega owner Usnavi changes his mind about fleeing his beloved but gentrifying neighborhood. Deciding to stay, he raps, "It's a Wonderful Life that I've known/Merry Christmas, you ole building and loan/I'm home!"

As the ensemble came out to the edge of the stage on the two-story set for their final bow, the Broadway audience erupted. "It was so loud and so beautiful," remembers Westcott. "People were cheering. It was this beautiful mix of older white subscribers and younger black and brown faces in the audience, people who were diehard mainstage audience members alongside people who had never heard of the Broadway Theatre or Pitman. Whether you're into hip-hop or not, 'In the Heights' is the story of community. That's what people responded to." Adds artistic director Heather Mattingley Grasso: "Watching an audience experience a roller coaster of emotions when you learn someone's story for the first time is one of the best things about what we do." Marketing manager Nick Blood was also gaining traction with younger theatregoers on the Broadway's Instagram account as actors from the Broadway musicals staged behind-the-scenes "takeovers" to engage with theatre fans.

In addition to the Broadway's resurging mainstage season, Darrell Blood was discovering strong audience response to the new lineup of tribute acts he was adding to the live concert calendar. With the real artists expired, retired or charging astronomical ticket prices, musical acts paying homage to the Rolling Stones, Boston, Aerosmith, Def Leppard, Journey, Elton John, Billy Joel, Frank Sinatra, Barbra Streisand, the Eagles, Van Halen, Liza Minnelli and even 1970s balladeer John Denver were pulling in hundreds of theatregoers each weekend.

"We play the Broadway annually, and it's my favorite gig of the year," says Whole Lotta AC/DC tribute band guitarist Drew Mancini. "It's a beautiful theatre and the people who run it make it feel like a family business." Whole Lotta AC/DC has become an audience favorite due to the authenticity of its stage show. In addition to its massive fake Marshall amps, the band rolls in a pair of "For Those About to Rock (We Salute You)" cannons and a massive "Hell's Bells" stage prop. The show's highlight is when the band shoots off the cannons onstage (in reality, sound effects and PVC piping attached to smoke machines tucked inside plastic cannon barrels).

At the back of the theatre, Mancini's teenage daughters sell red light-up devil horns at the merchandise table. "It's always wild to look out from the stage of this historic theatre and see this sea of devil horns and people having fun," says Mancini. The popularity of tribute bands doesn't surprise the guitarist. "A lot of people want to relive that AC/DC or that Van Halen show they went to at the Spectrum in Philly. But now they get to do it in a nice theatre with a comfortable seat. You're not standing up for hours with someone spilling beer on you. Plus, you're home for the 11 o'clock news."

Mancini and his Whole Lotta AC/DC bandmates will admit there's one drawback to playing a gig in Pitman — all the restaurants are jammed by the time they finish sound check. "Last year, we went to [Merryman's Pub] during our dinner break looking for a bite to eat and maybe a beer," recalls Mancini. "The place was completely mobbed. It was four deep at the bar. The hostess told us she didn't have a table available until 8:30, 30 minutes after we went on." A Merryman's regular then informed Mancini the massive crowd was due to "the band playing across the street." "That's when I noticed all of the people wearing the AC/DC shirts," Mancini says, laughing. "Then it dawned on me. Oh, *we're* the problem!"

*A Whole Lotta AC/DC tribute band performing
at the Broadway Theatre in 2024.*

Bill Haley Jr. & His Comets performing at the Broadway in 2023.

For longtime Pitmanite concertgoers like Ralph Richards Jr., one of the best shows booked there in recent memory wasn't technically a tribute act. Sixty-seven years after his father played Pitman's after-prom in 1956, Bill Haley Jr. & His Comets rocked the Broadway. Using vintage instruments, Haley Jr. and his band delivered authentic renditions of his dad's biggest hits, as photos and video clips from his father's career played on a screen over the stage. Introducing each number, Haley Jr. told the story behind "Rock Around the Clock" and his father's other hits.

"It's very cool when we're booked in a Pottstown [Pa.] or a Pitman where my dad played," says Haley Jr. "Playing a place like Pitman feels like you're touching a little piece of history. Thankfully, I sound pretty close to the original. Getting to perform for people who originally saw my father and seeing them smiling and clapping is really special. This music transports them back to their youth. It's incredibly rewarding for both the audience and me."

Like the two generational perspectives Ralph and Howard Wilkins brought to the Broadway working together a century ago, the theatre's current general manager, Darrell Blood and his son Nick sometimes have differing opinions on the venue's bookings. Take, for example, the Fearless Taylor Swift Experience tribute act the elder Blood booked in 2024.

"I thought it was completely ridiculous," says Nick Blood with a laugh. "The real performer is still out there doing shows. But I made sure I was in the house for the show. It turned out to be this really sweet mother-daughter experience. We ended up selling out two shows in 2024 and two more in 2025." Like Ralph Wilkins booking vaudeville acts at the Broadway 90 years ago, Darrell Blood has developed an innate sense of what will work on the modern Broadway stage.

Other acts that play surprisingly well in Pitman are the Calamari Sisters, two male actors in drag who play Delphine and Carmela Calamari, two Bay Ridge, Brooklyn, Italian sisters; and The Golden Gays, four drag queens performing a musical comedy show based on "The Golden Girls" sitcom. While the drag shows sell well (the Calamari Sisters have been a mainstay at the Broadway for more than a decade), occasionally a handful of Bible-toting protesters will gather outside (in June 2024, a single protester showed up with a huge unfurled Revelations verse posted on a pole).

"It's always the same small handful of people," says Nick Blood. "When they're out there, it can be unpleasant for the people trying to get into the theatre." In response to a 2021 protest, the Broadway placed speakers out front and played showstoppers from its mainstage productions. "It drowned out the protesters and it made the people coming in laugh," recalls Blood. "We used show tunes as our peaceful protest!"

One show booked for the Broadway's 2024 mainstage season featuring a drag queen lead character presented a particular challenge for older subscribers. On the show's opening weekend, the cast of the Broadway's next main-stage production paced anxiously backstage as they wondered just how "Kinky" Pitmanites were willing to get.

Kyle Smith as Lola and Blaze Dalio as Charlie in the 2024 production of "Kinky Boots." Photo by Zachary Moore. Courtesy of the Broadway Theatre.

CHAPTER TWELVE

"Not every building gets a second chance."
1926–2026

Charlie Price, the idealistic young protagonist of the Broadway musical "Kinky Boots," has a problem. He's the fourth-generation owner of a failing shoe factory in the small English town of Northampton. By the end of Act 1, Charlie has a decision to make — throw in with a headstrong drag queen named Lola and retrofit the factory to make stylish steel-reinforced footwear for men who perform in dresses. Or shutter the family business and sell the building.

Richard Bailey (played by A.J. Klein in the Broadway Theatre of Pitman's fall 2024 production) is hoping Charlie (Blaze Dalio) will choose the latter. Urging him to convert the antiquated structure into lucrative luxury condos, he tells Charlie, "Not every building gets a second chance."

Inside Pitman's historic 98-year-old theatre for the show's packed opening night on October 25, Charlie's decision to reinvent the space and keep his family's business alive resonated with the Broadway audience and its staff alike. At first blush, the title of the Tony-winning Cyndi Lauper/Harvey Fierstein musical on the Broadway marquee looked like something Duffy Platt might have booked at the Glassboro Theatre in 1973. But the show's themes of life-long bonds formed in a small town and embracing change made it a perfect fit for Pitman's growing subscriber base.

"I was excited to bring a show like 'Kinky Boots' to a town that might not have seen this story before or necessarily been around people who are LGBT or drag artists," says Lola's portrayer Kyle Smith. "Lola's story resonates a lot with me."

In addition to the show's uplifting theme, there was another practical reason to stage the 2013 musical at the Broadway. "We've done all of the classics, sometimes twice," explains Broadway general manager Darrell Blood. "You can't do 'Annie,' 'Oklahoma!' and 'The Sound of Music' forever. Staging newer shows brings in younger audiences, which we need in order to remain sustainable." Adds longtime director Drew Molotsky: "The Broadway did a great job of building a strong subscriber base by doing those meat-and-potatoes shows. But Rodgers and Hammerstein only wrote so many shows. At some point, you have to cultivate new audiences with subject matter relevant to the times." Still, a parade of drag queens proudly strutting across the Broadway stage in sequined stiletto boots during the show's spirited finale looked and felt gutsy in Pitman, N.J. But afterward, two of the mainstage series' 70-something subscribers excitedly discussing the show on the way to their car appeared unfazed. Walking past the old Bob's Hobbies space on Broadway, which has now been transformed into a popular antique shop, one of the women confided, "I didn't know anything about the show going in. But they always do great productions here. We used to go to the Walnut Street Theatre in Philly, but now we just come to Pitman."

"Every time we have ever challenged the Broadway Theatre of Pitman audiences, they have responded spectacularly well," says director Molotsky. As an actor, Kyrus Keenan Westcott knows when a Pitman audience has truly loved a performance. "Whenever you get a standing ovation at the Broadway, you've earned it, 100 percent. If people get out of their seats in Pitman, we know, 'Oh, we got 'em! They really liked this.'"

"'Rent' was the show that broke things open for the audience," says Nathan Figlio, who plays the mainstage preshows at the Kimball organ before sliding into a seat with his wife, Barbara, for at least one performance of each musical. "At the beginning, maybe it was eight or 10 subscribers who didn't want to see shows like this. Now it's one or two. Over the years, our audiences have embraced seeing something on our stage maybe they haven't experienced before. For me, that's what great theatre does. You know you're going to be safe at the Broadway with what gets put onstage."

Darrell Blood wasn't surprised by the favorable reaction to "Kinky Boots": "Pitman has progressed."

For evidence of that, visitors don't have to walk farther than the theatre's adjacent restaurant, Martini's on Broadway, with its full bar, cocktail list and entrees including short rib risotto and bang bang shrimp tacos. On show nights, the restaurant is so packed, reservations are a necessity. The scene is much the same at Merryman's Pub, where access to a bar stool is minimal when the theatre is open. In his own small way, former Pitman Mayor Andrew Trucksess, Duffy Platt's grandfather, had a role in Pitman's current successful status as a "wet" town. In 1933 Trucksess, a noted progressive, became one of the Gloucester County delegates who successfully circulated petitions to repeal Prohibition.

For a town founded by Methodists where not only alcohol but train stops on the Sabbath were once forbidden, the successful operation of two restaurants with full-service bars represents an enormous leap into the future. And in a borough where Sunday entertainment was illegal until 1970, the day now represents one of the busiest of the week for Pitman's business district.

Thanks to the popularity of the theatre's weekend shows, Broadway's other restaurants are also booming on show nights, including Sweet Lula's, Mannino's Wood-Fired Pizzeria, Nine Thai Cuisine, Ming Lok Chinese and Lucia's Bistro. The 2025 dining scene is a far cry from when Drew Molotsky began directing shows at the Broadway in 2009. "If I came out of a rehearsal after 6 p.m., the whole street was closed," he remembers. "Now there's a show at the Broadway 45 out of 52 weeks in the year. You have between five hundred and a thousand people a night in that theatre every weekend."

No one knows that better than real estate developer Brandon Hedenberg. "The theatre is our biggest economic driver. When the 1907 Hotel Pitman came down [in 2010] and four new houses went up in 2018, each sold for about $400,000, unheard-of numbers back then. Today, the single-family-home record has soared past $700,000 and the momentum keeps building."

Park Theatre, Pitman, N. J.

Tuesday Evening, Sept. 22

AN EXTRA FINE MOTION PICTURE SHOW

6--Reels of Best Pictures--6

2 Features of Two Parts Each and 2 Comedies

Also Tex D'Art & Co.

The Wonderful French Lightning Brush Artist

RAPID WATER COLOR SKETCHES AND LANDSCAPES, including a beautiful satin hand-painted pillow top to be given to the lady holding the lucky number for each performance. These pillow tops are worth seven dollars each, and are a beautiful work of art. He will give two performances, so that late comers will be enabled to enjoy his act as well as early ones. Come hear some good singing, also the latest illustrated song.

... Musical Programme ...

Overture	Dream-Waltz
Song	"Peg of My Heart"
Song	"When the Angelus Is Ringing"
Illustrated Song	"The Land of My Best Girl"
Song	"Meet Me at the Frisco Fair"

Show Starts at 7.15 sharp. Second Show Begins at 9

Prices for This Extra Fine Show:

Adults, 15c : : Children, 10c

Early-1920s Hunt's Park Theatre program. Photo courtesy of Brandon Hedenberg.

Hedenberg is so bullish on his hometown, he bought the building at 101 W. Jersey Ave., across from the railroad tracks where trains still come through town twice daily. During the 111-year-old building's extensive renovation, the young entrepreneur made an unexpected discovery. As workers were transforming the space into the new Hedenberg Real Estate Company, they uncovered the fading remains of a beautiful tin ceiling – and a stack of old flyers. The yellowed advertisements were promoting an appearance by Tex D'Art, "the wonderful French lightning brush artist," along with "an extra fine motion picture show with six reels of the best pictures. Adults: 15 cents, Children 10 cents." After a quick consult with Pitman native Mike Doughty – administrator for the "Old Images of Pitman" Facebook page – the 27-year-old realized he was the new owner of Pitman's first silent movie house, the Hunt's Park.

"I had no idea about its history," says Hedenberg. "I just wanted to bring the building back to life. As we started doing our own research, I became enthralled with learning more." To pay tribute to the historic building's past, one of the colorized Hunt's Park Theatre photos Doughty sent over has been enlarged and now hangs on the conference room wall of the fully restored building. In honor of the theatre's original look, a new tin ceiling has also been installed.

Another native Pitmanite who was surprised by the building's revelations? Broadway Theatre owner Peter Slack, who as a high schooler got paid $1.25 an hour to clean the West Jersey Avenue address after hours. In the 1960s and into the 1970s, the building served as company headquarters for Charles B. Slack Inc., his father's medical publishing company. That business is now owned and operated by Peter Slack as The Wyanoke Group in West Deptford. "I guess our family is more connected to Pitman theatres than I knew," says Slack. "I never knew my dad's old building had been a theatre!"

Back at 43 S. Broadway, the theatre's mainstage subscribers continue to embrace change. Director Drew Molotsky, who directed "Mary Poppins" there in 2020, returned in March 2025 to helm "Jersey Boys," the jukebox musical celebrating the life and career of Frankie Valli and the Four Seasons. "On opening night we were a little anxious," concedes Gary Schneider, the show's orchestra coordinator. "There's F-bombs dropping all over the place in this show." Adds Molotsky: "When I started here in 2009, that was an absolute no-no. The F-bomb was absolutely out of the question. We would have to seek special permission from [the theatrical-rights reps] not to say those words. But with 'Jersey Boys,' we give the same warning at the top of the show they gave on Broadway — 'This show uses authentic New Jersey language.' The audiences laugh out loud. We're doing thousand-seat sellouts. It's a different world."

Its success over the last 20 years as a live stage for Broadway musicals notwithstanding, if you ask older Pitmanites to recount their fondest memories of the Broadway Theatre, their recollections always begin in childhood — on Saturday afternoons. "For 25 cents you could see Roy Rogers, Dale Evans and Hopalong Cassidy," remembers native Joan Schaeffer Eldredge. "I went with my sister Barbara. There were newsreels and cartoons before the features. It lasted all afternoon. We saved our allowance to go. When I was growing up, there was a penny candy store on Broadway and you could get a whole bag for 25 cents! We'd sneak that into the theatre with us. It was a place you could go without your parents."

In Jason Weber's 2006 documentary, John Wilkins, grandson of the Broadway's first owner-operator, Ralph Wilkins, recalled his granddad attempting to keep order during Saturday matinees full of small fry. "Whenever it got too wild and crazy in the theatre, my grandfather would stand up on a seat and go [cupping his hands over his mouth] 'QUIET!!' And suddenly, the entire theatre would be hushed. But kids being kids, the minute he walked back up the aisle, the roar started all over again."

"We were animals!" concedes Ray Biddle, laughing. The Spokane, Washington, filmmaker would be introduced to the Three Stooges and "Willy Wonka and the Chocolate Factory" at the Broadway. "Old man Platt would stand in the back of the theatre watching us like a hawk. What poor employee had the job of cleaning up after us?! It took me until the age of 13 to learn to be respectful in there."

"We would do odd jobs to get the money to go to the matinee," says Mike Doughty, whose first memory of the Broadway is seeing "101 Dalmatians" there. "There was a freedom in being able to walk to the theatre without your parents. Back in the early 1970s, none of our houses were air-conditioned, so going to the Broadway was a great way to get out of the heat in the middle of the summer." Adds Carmen Cattafi: "It almost didn't matter what was playing. We were 12-year-old boys goofing around. It was a chance to group up with your friends, get some popcorn, candy and soda and have a good time."

Ralph J. Richards Jr., who compiled the Images of America "Pitman" book with Michael D. Batten Jr., remembers paying a 10-cent admission on Saturdays as a boy — if he got caught. "My friends and I always tried to walk in backwards so Mr. Wilkins thought we were leaving!" says Richards. "But by the time I was 10, I was almost 6 foot tall, so I couldn't sneak in *anywhere* anymore."

Former Pitman councilwoman Debra Moore Higbee can still recite her Saturday-morning ritual as a girl. "My friends and I would go around with a wagon and collect bottles in our neighborhood. We got a nickel for some, pennies for others. We kept at it until we each had a quarter to get into the matinee and a nickel to put into the candy machine. Then we would all traipse off to the Broadway. If people were misbehaving, Mr. Wilkins would appear and the offenders were removed. Mr. Wilkins kept order." Except for one particular Saturday afternoon around 1960 when an incident occurred that has become legendary around the borough. "I was 10 or 11 at the time," recalls Higbee. "Suddenly we saw this football get thrown from the balcony and it went completely through the movie screen! I knew the kid who did it and I asked him about it later and he said, 'I always wondered if I threw a football, would it go through the screen.' They mended it, but for years whenever you watched a movie at the Broadway, you could see the patch."

While much has changed in Pitman over the Broadway Theatre's 100 years, if you look hard enough, many remnants of the town's history remain. The White Star Laundry whistle that blew on V.E. Day and V.J. Day signaling the end of World War II is now on display at the Pitman Historical Museum in the Pitman Grove. It rests a few feet from the surviving pulpit pulled from Pitman United Methodist Church after the devastating 2003 fire. The land where the century-old church once stood on Broadway is now a parking lot. The PUMC's mission statement, painted by long-time member Bill Lanning, now hangs inside the rebuilt church's current home, down the street at Broadway and Lambs Road. The manual Underwood typewriter that once belonged to Pitman Grove Review contributor Len Eckman, who wrote whimsically about cooking schools and Miss Pitman pageants at the Broadway, is also in the museum's permanent collection. Overhead is the Cobbin Jewelry clock, rescued from the shop following its tragic 1968 fire.

Outside the museum, the small, meticulously maintained gingerbread-trim Grove summer cottages also remain. Many of them, now over 100 years old, were built on the 12 avenues that ring the Pitman Grove Auditorium, where summer prayer services are still held. In 2025, the few cottages for sale (many of which are less than 900 square feet) were fetching upwards of $230,000.

Entrance to the Pitman Grove, summer 2024.

Up First Avenue, the former Pitman National Bank now hosts karaoke nights and "Dinner With the Grinch" holiday events for kids in its current incarnation as Merryman's Pub. The space next door to the Broadway, which previously housed an Acme supermarket and Community Appliances, is now Martini's on Broadway. Meanwhile, the retail spaces and apartments envisioned in 1925 by W.A. Lacy as part of the block-long Broadway Theatre complex are still being used a century later, notably now as the home of Pitman Pharmacy. Theatre Avenue, where buses carrying country stars like Tammy Wynette and Johnny Cash once arrived, is now Theatre Plaza, a pocket park filled with strings of lights overhead, tables, chairs and families eating ice cream from the nearby Crazy Kat Dessertery.

On a Sunday afternoon, 30 minutes before the 2 p.m. matinee, the Broadway's marketing manager, Nicholas

Blood, is busy distributing "Kinky Boots" tickets through the box office window. For him, the theatre isn't just his workplace. It's where he spent weekends as a 10-year-old learning Elvis songs by watching tribute performer Doug Church onstage and helping to paint the sets for musicals. Hoping to get the Broadway even more involved in the community, Blood has joined the town's chamber of commerce. "I guess I could be working in New York or somewhere else doing marketing," he reasons. "But I feel like I'm having more impact right here. Besides, it's fun. This is literally my second home. You get the bug and you want to help out." Seated on a stool, taking tickets at the door, the Broadway's now-retired painter Walter Madison occasionally pauses to admire his handiwork. "Sometimes when I go into a show, I'll sit there staring and think, 'I can't believe I did this.' Part of me still can't quite grasp it. If not for Pete Slack, I can't imagine where this town would be without this theatre."

As patrons file into the auditorium, Kimball organist Nathan Figlio, clad in his signature cowboy hat, is in the middle of his preshow concert. "This is my version of church," Figlio says wistfully. "My 'ministry' of organ music ... is to make it as accessible as possible. I've played Queen, Santana and the themes to 'Popeye the Sailor Man' and 'Casper the Friendly Ghost.' My repertoire covers the entire 100 years of the theatre. I feel so blessed that I get to do this in the place where I grew up listening to my dad play the same instrument. Every time I play now, it feels like spending 30 minutes with him." Now with his sheet music loaded onto an iPad, Nathan has a ritual that honors his father, Robert M. Figlio. He always closes his set with his dad's arrangements of "I Can't Believe You're in Love With Me" and "The Perfect Song." As Figlio cranks the Kimball's volume and plays his father's signature runup at the end, the cast and crew throughout the building know that's their cue to take their places.

On the other side of the wall, Keith David Brown, who grew up in the theatre watching "Finding Nemo" and acting in the children's summer theatre camp, is working the concession stand. "Aesthetically, it's such a gorgeous environment to work in and I get to hear Nathan play. It's such a marvelous, evocative sound." Adds Keith's dad, James Brown, who grew up being scared by Hammer horror flicks at the Broadway: "I love that this theatre will continue into the future, not only during my life but for Keith's life. It will remain a part of our community."

Just before walking onstage to deliver her remarks as the Broadway's producing artistic director, Heather Mattingley Grasso reflects on her journey at the performing arts venue where she debuted in 2009 as Peter Pan. "Being able to literally fly in a theatre like the Broadway was beyond magical. You never forget the beauty of the building, its ambience or the people you get to create that magic with. Our goal here is to take you to Neverland each time you step inside these doors."

For audience members who have never been exposed to an episode of "RuPaul's Drag Race," Lola – the force-of-nature drag queen shoe designer from "Kinky Boots" – can initially come across as downright scary. But by the time Lola's portrayer Kyle Smith and the show's 24-person cast hit the final notes of the rousing electronic-dance-music finale, "Raise You Up/Just Be," the Sunday-matinee crowd has been raised up out of its seats. "When Lola wins over the audience, it's a really special moment," reflects Smith.

"Especially since this is a show that humanizes queer people and people of color. It was really emotional seeing how warm and receptive the Pitman audiences were, especially with the climate of the world right now. It reminded us that there is still love, hope and acceptance present in the world. And there's a place for people like me and for everyone on that stage to exist."

Jeff Sanders, former councilman and a founding member of the Pitman Economic Development Committee, isn't insulted when a new visitor compares Pitman, "The Small Town With a Big Heart," to a Norman Rockwell painting or Hallmark movie set. After all, "It's a Wonderful Life" remains his favorite film for a reason — Bedford Falls reminds him of his favorite small town. "We're the envy of every other town in Gloucester County, many of whom are spending millions of dollars to build a town center like ours," says Sanders. "Yes, we're always going to have people complaining about parking. I like to say Pitman doesn't have a parking problem, we have a *walking* problem. I tell people, without the success of the theatre, you would have your pick of open parking spaces on Broadway."

Admits former Mayor Russell Johnson: "Sometimes I even do it myself — I'll be driving down Broadway cursing because I can't find a place to park. And then my wife reminds me, 'Why are you cursing? This is what you wanted!' I recently went to the ABBA tribute show at the theatre. I was sitting there with a cocktail in my hand inside a packed 99-year-old theatre. I just remember thinking, 'Holy shit, who would have thought this was possible?!' It was just surreal. We used to feel like we had to compete with Deptford Mall. Now, Deptford Mall has to compete with *us*."

Still writing and recording at age 79, Donna Fargo remains proud of helping to usher in the era of Pitman Country at the Broadway in 1977. "I don't know that I was really responsible for anything," she says. "Mr. Platt got all that going. Those amazing performers would have done well anywhere. Who's better than Johnny Cash, Tom T. Hall, Loretta Lynn and Tammy Wynette? The Broadway was one of my favorites to play. I just remember Pitman being a special place and those audiences were very special to me."

Pitman native Debra Moore Higbee, vice chair of the Pitman Historic Preservation Commission, feels comfort and gratitude when she walks into the theatre now. "It's just something we've always done and a place our kids always went. Even in its worst years, we still went to the Broadway. We are so fortunate that this beautiful building is still here." Higbee's fellow former borough council member and Pitman High educator Paul Blass adds, "Theatre, historically, has always brought people together. In the silent era when the Broadway debuted, immigrants who couldn't yet understand English could still understand the language of silent cinema. Class and other societal differences faded in the dark as people came together to sit and watch a show and be lost in it next to each other for a couple of hours. That aspect of the theatre's importance hasn't changed in 100 years. It remains valuable." Says San Francisco filmmaker and former Broadway projectionist Ken Paul Rosenthal: "The experience of sitting in that space is at least as important as whatever is onstage. Those old theatres were built like huge living rooms, meant for you to be comfortable, yet it was constructed to be collectively comfortable. It's a communal experience. I'm not at all surprised the Broadway is still enjoying success. After the pandemic, where everyone became a couch potato for two years, we crave those collective experiences again."

"Every time I walk into the Broadway, I feel like a little kid again," says Ralph Richards Jr. "I'm about to turn 80. I can't say that about too many places. You'd wait in line to get into the auditorium and you'd look at the coming-attractions posters and decide which ones you were going to see and which ones you weren't. I was sitting in there early before a concert with my son recently and the house lights were still up. My son turned to me and said, 'This place is so beautiful. You're not going to see places like this built again.'" Adds former Broadway staffer and Pitman councilman Kevin Austin: "The story of the Broadway is evolution and its ability to change to survive. We owe all of the Broadway's owners a debt of gratitude. For 100 years, they all kept it up and running. It's still here. As I used to say when I was on council, 'If the business district dies, the town dies.'"

Still living downtown, former Broadway owner Daniel Munyon and his wife, Mary Ann, are pleased to see the theatre doing well, even if it presents challenges trying to get in their front door with groceries on performance nights. Dan Munyon continues to share his love of classic films by screening them at local senior communities via Movie Man Ministries, a nonprofit he started in 2019. "I still get to connect with people who love these movies and put smiles on their faces," says Munyon. Summing up the life lessons the Broadway provided during his six-year run as owner-operator, Munyon concedes with a laugh, "You have to be a little off to want to own a movie theatre. But I'm pleased to be a part of its history. There have only been four of us. I was one of the caretakers. History is very important to me – just ask my grandchildren. My legacy at the Broadway is the people and how they enjoyed themselves there. I gave kids a safe place to be. I did it for them." Munyon laughs and adds, "Even the kids who somehow snuck into the theatre one night with a pizza!"

Pitman native Mike Doughty feels the town's reinvigorated energy every time he walks his dog uptown. "We've now got 100,000 people coming into town a year, essentially 10 times the town's population. Walking into the Broadway feels like stepping back into your childhood. But now, as an adult, it's even better. You can go next door to Martini's, have a drink and dinner and then go to the show." Carmen Cattafi, who works a few yards away at McCowan Memorial Library, reflects, "On Saturdays, on the way in or out of the children's programming at the theatre, I watch the families come into the library or the ice cream shop or the bookstore. I've never seen Pitman filled with so many families and happy kids. It's a beautiful success story."

Up the street, standing at his plate glass front window on West Jersey Avenue inside the old Hunt's Park Theatre building, real estate developer Brandon Hedenberg can survey the busy streetscape looking toward Broadway. "What we're seeing right now in Pitman is unparalleled in real estate," he says. "Other South Jersey communities like Haddonfield have downtowns like ours, but we're the only one with a gem like the Broadway Theatre. In real estate terms, you can draw a through-line between today's market and when Peter Slack purchased the theatre in 2006." Across Broadway at Merryman's Pub, William Merryman says that struggling through a lengthy and expensive renovation of the Pitman National Bank and then a global pandemic was worth the financial risks. "Five years later, the influence this town is having on everything around it is amazing. The Broadway Theatre started the ball rolling. It is without a doubt the number one downtown in Gloucester County. No one can compete with this right now."

As a kid, Pitman Mayor Michael L. Razze Jr. experienced the excitement of country stars rolling into town on their buses and eras of vacant storefronts. He's thrilled the theatre's 100th will be celebrated during his second term in office. "At borough hall, we talk about Pitman as a place of progress with relative frequency," says Razze. "We continue to evolve as society evolves. But we're also a community that has never lost touch with our roots and our core values. We're all connected, we're all neighbors here in these two square miles."

Ken Wilkins, great-grandson of the Broadway's first owner-operator, Ralph Wilkins, is delighted the theatre has beaten the odds. "All of us thought at some point, the theatre just wasn't going to be there anymore. It was going to end up like so many other small-town movie theatres – it just wouldn't work economically anymore and it would become a Planet Fitness or something. But the people in Pitman made the difference. I know my great-grandfather would be pleased that the theatre he dedicated so much of his life to is thriving and Pitman along with it." Adds Ken's mother, Bobbi Wilkins: "Pop-Pop would especially be pleased that the stage is still in use 100 years later. And because he did so much for the children of Pitman, he would love the family Christmas shows and the children's summer theatre camps now being held there."

Susan Lanning Crispin, who played the Kimball organ as Miss Pitman and has gone on to direct the town pageant at the theatre, has a unique vantage point on the Broadway's centennial. "Not only does this theatre go back to my childhood, but it goes back to my father's childhood, when he sat in the audience on opening night in 1926. Every time I sit in the balcony and see those beautiful crystal chandeliers, it's so majestic. It takes you back to another time. You can almost hear the voices of the past in there."

Twenty years on, as the Broadway's general manager in addition to his full-time role as CFO at Wyanoke Group, Darrell Blood is still enjoying his career's unexpected detour running a century-old theatre. "It's fun, it makes money and we can cover payroll, so it's all good. That's why you run a theatre. You don't do it to become a billionaire. You do it for the love of the arts and you do it for the town to do well."

In 2006, Peter Slack envisioned buying the Broadway, getting his hometown's business district on its feet and then donating or selling what he considered at the time to be an impulse purchase. It hasn't quite worked out that way. Moments after buying the Broadway, a reporter at the sheriff's sale asked Slack what he knew about running a movie theatre and he replied, "Nothing, but I've got good advisors." Twenty years later, Slack concedes with a chuckle, "Time goes pretty quick, doesn't it? I helped the town out and it worked. The town is in great shape. It was not the intention to own the theatre this long. We just wanted to get things started. It's been a funny ride. It really is amazing that we're doing this 20 years later."

At 90, Warren Carr has been around just a decade shy of the Broadway's tenure in town. The house he grew up in behind the theatre, with its distinctive 1909 stonework, still stands as a multifamily residence on Simpson Avenue. "I still enjoy going to see shows at the Broadway when I can manage to get tickets," says Carr. "With the Pitman National Bank building still there serving the community and the theatre doing well, it feels like a part of my family's legacy is still there, alive on Broadway. I think my grandfather would be very proud of what downtown Pitman has become and his very small role in helping to make Pitman what it is today."

The portrait of Dr. Henry H. Carr, that hangs in grandson Warren Carr's dining room.
Photo courtesy of Warren Carr.

The grandson of Dr. Henry H. Carr and the grandnephew of George W. Carr pauses for a moment when asked a final question: What's the legacy of the Broadway Theatre?

"Putting it rather bluntly, other than the churches, the theatre is the very center of the town," says Warren Carr. "All of the business, visitors, residents and all of the economic activity revolve around the Broadway Theatre. A full century after its construction, its location, its purpose and its influence remain. And the town of Pitman and its citizens remain the beneficiary of that economic activity. That's your answer."

BROADWAY
BROADWAY
THE PROM JULY 5 THROUGH JULY 28
BROADWAY
BROADWAY
PROM
July 5 - July 28, 2024
P

EXT: THE BROADWAY THEATRE

43 S. BROADWAY

PITMAN, NEW JERSEY

TIME: AFTERNOON

JULY 6, 2024

The line to get into Martini's on Broadway to sample its brunch menu, complete with a champagne mimosa, now extended out onto the sidewalk. Across the street at Words Matter bookshop, the Sunday Silent Book Club meeting had made way for an afternoon of browsers milling about the store. Inside the converted circa-1911 Pitman National Bank, visitors and locals were two deep conversing at the Merryman's Pub bar while sampling Swoosh IPA drafts from local brewery Bonesaw.

With the last spot on Broadway long since taken, patrons arriving for the 2 p.m. matinee streamed in from the parking lot on West Holly Avenue, the lot Ralph Wilkins helped to create in 1940. Inside the Broadway Theatre, mainstage subscribers ordered cocktails and grabbed popcorn as they were escorted to their seats by ushers. Backstage, the cast members of "The Prom" were attaching their microphone headsets and making final costume adjustments.

The 2018 Broadway musical centers on a quartet of narcissistic New York actors from the flop musical "Eleanor! The Eleanor Roosevelt Story" who invade a small Indiana town in search of an Instagram-worthy cause célèbre to rebuild their public images. They find one in high school student Emma Nolan, who has been banned from attending her school prom with her closeted summer-Bible-camp-attending girlfriend Alyssa Greene.

Given what had transpired on the show's opening night, the "Prom" cast – a diverse ensemble of mostly younger performers, who'd worked for months to bring the show to life – are a little anxious. At the show's premiere in Pitman, one mainstage subscriber had stormed out of the theatre. Ironically, the eruption occurred at the comical conclusion of "The Acceptance Song," as 6-foot rainbow flags unfurled from the skirt of Brooke Birbilis, who was portraying Angie Dickinson, the lovable Broadway hoofer, in the show. Onstage, the cast witnessed the commotion. Spotting the upset audience member, Broadway artistic director Heather Mattingley Grasso guided her out into the lobby. Pointing a finger in Grasso's face, the enraged subscriber told her, "You should be ashamed of yourself! I didn't come here to be lectured to or to see a message!" Recalls Grasso: "I asked her, 'Then why *did* you come? Every show we stage has a message, whether it's 'The Prom,' 'The Little Mermaid' or 'Ragtime.' It's not always going to be your story up there.' She was livid. Finally I said, 'There's the door.'"

When the perspiring ensemble came offstage, Grasso and director Drew Molotsky were waiting in the wings. "They gathered us all together to tell us how proud they were of us and how the incident illustrated the importance of us telling this story," says actor Kyrus Keenan Westcott, who played Principal Hawkins in the show. Explains Grasso: "My job is to make sure our actors feel comfortable. If they doubt themselves walking out on that stage playing these characters, then we have a different show."

Adds Broadway organist Nathan Figlio: "Yes, the musical is about two girls who want to go to the prom together. But any adult who experienced the challenges of being a teenager in high school can identify with the show."

Afterward, the cast gathered across the street at the Brewed Awakening Café to sample the coffee shop's brand-new "Prom"-inspired iced dark chocolate and raspberry "Love Latte" and "Prom Punch," a hibiscus tea layered with blue raspberry lemonade and glitter. A few doors away, the Crazy Kat had baked "Prom Night"-themed cupcakes for theatregoers.

Throughout the show's rehearsals in June, the cast and creative team entered and exited the theatre on a street covered in rainbow banners erected for Pride month, courtesy of the borough and the Pride Alliance of Pitman. The cast was further reminded of the theatre's support when general manager Darrell Blood sent them an email following the opening-night incident, stating, "You're doing a great job, keep doing what you're doing." When the show was announced earlier in the year, Blood had fielded a few phone calls from individuals with the same mindset as the opening-night subscriber. Blood's suggested solution was simple: "'If this show isn't your cup of tea, give your tickets to someone who will enjoy it and we'll see you at the next production.'" Of Blood's email, Grasso says, "I never felt as at home at the Broadway as I did in that moment. It meant everything to the cast."

A few minutes past 2 p.m., performing against a swirl of brightly colored school lockers onstage, Jill Saperstein, the young actress playing Emma, took a deep breath and sang her first number. "Note to self/Don't be gay in Indiana/Big heads up/That's a really stupid plan/There are places where it's in to be out/Maybe San Francisco or thereabout/But in Indiana without a doubt/If you're not straight then guess what's about to hit the fan?/Just breathe, Emma/Not everyone is that repressed/Just breathe, Emma/It wouldn't be high school without a test."

For veteran Pitmanites, the pop culture punchlines in the script play like a greatest hits of the Broadway Theatre's biggest moments over the last century. There are references to "The Wizard of Oz," Mickey Rooney and Judy Garland, "Beauty and the Beast," "Evita" and even jokes centering on a "Last Temptation of Christ" Broadway musical.

But for director Drew Molotsky, the most anxiety-inducing moment was seeing how the humorously biting "Love Thy Neighbor" number would play in a small town founded by Methodists 119 years earlier as a summer camp. "It's the one scene, based on where we're staging the show, where I thought we might lose people," says Molotsky. The gospel-tinged ensemble number, led by "non-Equity 'Godspell'" actor Trent Oliver and the town's high schoolers, hilariously exposes the hypocrisy of cherry-picking from the Bible.

Flying around the Broadway stage as Trent, veteran BTOP actor Vinnie DiFilippo sings, "There's no way to separate/Which rules you can violate/Let's hope you don't masturbate/'Cause the scripture says we'll have to cut off your ... hands/Or we could use some common sense instead

/When you're lost, it always helps recalling/Those immortal words that Jesus said/There's one rule that trumps them all/Love thy neighbor!"

Two-and-a-half hours later, with Emma and Alyssa finally reunited onstage inside a historic theatre that hosted prom-night celebrations for decades, the entire ensemble gathers for the show's joyous finale, "It's Time to Dance." Moving in unison to Billy D. Hart's choreography, the 23-member cast sings, "It's time to build a prom/For everyone/Show them all/It can be done/If music blares/And no one cares/Who your unruly heart loves/Build it now/Make people see/How the world/Could one day be/It might come true/If we take a chance/It's time to dance!"

At the climax of the finale, the back wall of the set flies out to reveal the 11-person orchestra playing on a platform above the stage as confetti cannons shoot streamers out across the stage and into the audience.

An audience that is already out of its seats, applauding and cheering.

Photo courtesy of Pitman Historical Museum.

Acknowledgments

Thanks, first and foremost to Mike Doughty and the nearly 8,000 members of the "Old Images of Pitman" Facebook group. I could not even have contemplated tackling a century's worth of history without your enthusiastic support, endless knowledge and active participation. Special thanks to Nancy Borrell for supplying the email that got this entire project started. I'm grateful to Peter and Jill Slack and Darrell Blood for meeting with me at the Broadway in February 2024, giving me a tour and offering insights and encouragement throughout the research and writing process. Gail Persa at Cresse and Carr for kindly facilitating many communications with Warren Carr. Debra Moore Higbee for opening up the Pitman Historical Museum archives to me and for ensuring I got the story of the Broadway and Pitman as factually accurate as possible. I am deeply indebted to Barbara Price and Karen Brisson at the Gloucester County Historical Society Library, where I spent a month over the course of a year researching and scrolling through old newspapers on microfilm and sifting through voluminous archives. Your endless expertise is reflected in these pages.

Thanks also to Daniel Munyon for trusting me with your piece of the Broadway story and for sharing your many images and memories. I am most grateful. Carmen Cattafi at

McCowan Memorial Library for facilitating Saturday interview sessions with residents. Within the walls of that library, I dreamed of becoming a writer. It was an incredibly powerful experience to return there to do reporting for this book. I thank you. BTOP marketing manager Nick Blood for answering every pesky email, offering your insights and for successfully positioning our beloved Broadway for its next successful century. For Walt Madison and Heather Grasso, for being the kind and accommodating first and final interviews for this book and the 40 other folks who graciously sat for the interviews that bring this book to life. I am grateful. Special thanks to my former neighbors Dorothy Neuman Cooper, Kirsten Sooy DiPatri, Margaret Jacobs and DonaLee Shirley Milner, who have miraculously come back into my life as a result of this project. I'm also grateful to my former Summit Avenue kindergarten classmates Jonathan Sayer and Joseph Chauncy for their encouragement.

Pitman Mayor Michael L. Razze Jr. for your participation and encouragement and for agreeing to write a wonderful introduction. Pitman Economic Development Committee co-founder Jeff Sanders for offering wisdom and being a one-man cheerleading squad for this project. Bill Merryman for his help and a shared love of Pitman's fascinating history. Broadway organist Nathan Figlio, for two generations' worth of insights, and for sharing vintage recordings of the Broadway Kimball organ in action and hilarious texts that helped rally this book to completion. Ralph Richards, for sharing insights, photos and vintage programs.

To all of the businesses that helped nourish this book into the world, including Brewed Awakening Café (the official coffee shop of this book!), Pitman indie acoustic duo AFTYN for providing the perfect soundtrack to edit by, Uptown Antiques, Words Matter Books, Pitman Pastries, Merryman's Pub, Attilio's Pizza, Ming Lok, Mi Familia II, Nine Thai Cuisine, the Monarch Diner and of course, Martini's on Broadway. May the entire world experience your hospitality and the restorative power of Old-Fashioned Burger Night, all under the watchful eye of George Bailey.

My family and friends: My dear aunt Joan Eldredge, who at 92 is an inspiration; Ralph and Diane Eldredge, for the text message that resulted in this book; and my father, Lee, and stepmother, Ann Foeste-Eldredge, for their love, support and for understanding why this book was important to me. A special thank you to friend and science reporter Maryn McKenna for the background on the 1919 Spanish flu outbreak and the resulting Fresh Air Movement. My bestie and 35-year editor Krista Reese for sage editorial feedback. To our brilliant writer and poet friend Susan O'Dell Underwood for taking the time to write a blurb and for understanding why this small-town story matters. Copy editor E.A. Axelberg for offering an exquisite eye and for kindly kicking my butt until this manuscript was fit for human consumption. This book is better because of you. Huge thanks to Ardmore Avenue Publishing co-founder and Chief Creative Director Paolo Aguila for the gorgeous design of this book.

Finally, thanks go to this project's most valuable player, Warren H. Carr, who sat for multiple interviews, took endless phone calls and dispensed wisdom and great humor onto every page of this book, including the foreword. You are this book's living link to 100 years of Broadway Theatre and Pitman history. I am eternally grateful to you for sharing both your time and your personal and professional reflections for this book.

S O U R C E S
Interviews conducted by the author

Walter J. Madison

Warren H. Carr

Brandon Hedenberg

Michael L. Razze Jr.

Tammy DeLucas Razze

Kevin Austin

Ralph J. Richards Jr.

Michael D. Batten Jr.

Russell Johnson

William Merryman

Debra Moore Higbee

Jane McCausland

Gary Schneider

Drew Molotsky

Kyrus Keenan Westcott

Daniel Munyon

Kyle Smith

Peter Slack

Jill Slack

Darrell Blood

Nicholas Blood

Jeff Sanders

Lee Eldredge

Joan Schaeffer Eldredge

Ken Paul Rosenthal

Ray Biddle

James C Brown

Keith David Brown

Nathan Figlio

Ken Wilkins

Bobbi Wilkins

Paul Blass

Mike Doughty

Carmen Cattafi

Susan Lanning Crispin

Bill Haley Jr.

Drew Mancini

Donna Fargo

George Burns (1992)

Loretta Lynn (2002, 2008)

Heather Mattingley Grasso

Acknowledgments

ARCHIVES

Pitman Historical Museum, Pitman, NJ

Gloucester County Historical Society Library, Woodbury, NJ

Philadelphia Architects and Buildings Project, | Philadelphia, PA

Athenaeum of Philadelphia, Philadelphia, PA

Broadway Theatre of Pitman, Pitman, NJ

Gloucester County Real Estate Records via 20/20 Perfect Vision Land Records

PERIODICALS

The Woodbury Daily Times

Gloucester County Times

South Jersey Times

Courier-Post

Gloucester County Democrat

Camden Evening Courier

Vineland Journal

Camden Daily Courier

Bridgeton Pioneer

Pitman Grove Review

Philadelphia Inquirer

Camden Morning Post

The Review, Cam-Glo Newspapers

NJ Advance Media

Box Office magazine

08071 magazine

Pitman Broadway Theatre programs, 1928 to 1970

Broadway Theatre of Pitman playbills, 2007 to 2025

BOOKS

"Cottagers and Commuters: A History of Pitman, NJ," by Harold F. Wilson, 1955

"Cottagers and Commuters: A History of Pitman, NJ," by Harold F. Wilson and Lorraine Allison Mollenhauer, updated, 1975

"Pitman: A Town for All Seasons",
Heritage of Pitman Committee, 1979

Images of America "Pitman" by Michael D. Batten Jr. and Ralph J. Richards Jr., 2002

Images of America "South Jersey Movie Houses," by Allen F. Hauss, 2006

Images of America "Glassboro" by Robert W. Sands Jr., 2004

Images of America "Woodbury" by Robert W. Sands Jr. and Barbara L. Turner with the Gloucester County Historical Society, 2006

Pitman's Centennial Celebration 2005 Official Program by Pitman Centennial Committee, 2005

"The Story of Pitman and a Plea for Rural Life," by Prof. William MacFarland, issued by the Pitman Board of Trade, 1907

First Congressional District of New Jersey, Volume II, 1900

DVDS/BLURAYS

"Pitman, New Jersey: The Centennial Celebration," Grover Productions, 2005

"Behind The Front," 1926, Paramount Pictures

"The Vanishing American," 1926, Paramount Pictures

"Ben-Hur: A Tale of the Christ," Metro Goldwyn-Mayer, 1925

"What Do You Say to a Naked Lady?" United Artists/MGM, 1970

"Waterfront" TV series, Collection 1, 1954, 2015

DIGITAL

Excerpts from Miss Pitman pageant 1986, YouTube

"Here It Is, Burlesque," HBO, 1979, YouTube

Larry Ferrari, WPVI-TV, 1982, Parts 1 and 2, YouTube

"Rebuilding The Broadway" documentary by filmmaker Jason Weber, 2006, YouTube

Broadway Theatre of Pitman Pre-Restoration footage by James C. Brown, 2006, YouTube

Esther Higgins on the Kimball Organ at the Pitman Broadway Theatre, March 1, 1970, private collection of Robert M. Figlio and Nathan Figlio

Lowell Ayres on the Kimball Organ at the Pitman Broadway Theatre, February 22, 1970, private collection of Robert M. Figlio and Nathan Figlio

RECORDINGS

Larry Ferrari on the Kimball Organ at the Pitman Broadway Theatre, April 19, 1970, private collection of Robert M. Figlio and Nathan Figlio

About the Author

Author Richard L. Eldredge is an Atlanta-based arts reporter and fourth-generation Pitmanite who saw his first film, "Disney's The Jungle Book," at the Broadway. He has been in love with storytelling and his hometown theatre ever since.